D0246223

THIS BOOK BELONGS TO
....

To Aaron. Let's go on an adventure.

E.J.

To Isabel Losada - the 'Joyful Environmentalist' who gave me the leaf confetti activity!

A.W.

First published 2021 by Nosy Crow Ltd.
The Crow's Nest, 14 Baden Place, Crosby Row
London SE1 1YW
www.nosycrow.com

ISBN 978 1 78800 994 2

A CIP catalogue record for this book is available from the British Library.

Printed in China

Papers used by Nosy Crow are made from wood grown in sustainable forests.

1 3 5 7 9 8 6 4 2

2022 NATURE MONTH-BY-MONTH

A Children's Almanac

Anna Wilson

Elly Jahnz

WHAT IS AN ALMANAC?

The first almanacs were created about 3,000 years ago! They were written by the ancient Egyptians, who used a kind of paper made from reeds known as papyrus. The writers listed all the dates that were thought to be lucky or unlucky, and made predictions about the weather. Farmers used these almanacs to help them know when to plant seeds and when to harvest crops.

Nowadays you can also find almanacs (like this one!) which have fun facts about each month – things to do indoors and outdoors, animals to spot, festivals to celebrate and seasonal food to grow, cook and eat. They also contain information about the weather, the night sky and all sorts of other amazing facts.

WARNING!

This book contains activities which involve things like knives, saws, hammers and nails and hot ovens. There are also a lot of fun things to do outside which involve fire and very cold water! All the activities are safe if you are sensible, follow safety guidelines and take a grown-up along to look out for you.

CONTENTS

JANUARY

SPECIAL DAYS

1st New Year's Day/First-footing
5th Twelfth Night/Wassailing
6th Epiphany
13th Lohri (Punjabi midwinter festival)
17th Tu B'Shevat (Jewish New Year)
25th Burns Night

ANNIVERSARIES

30 years ago . . .

On 1 January 1992, Jocelyn Barrow became the first black woman to be made a dame (DBE) in the Queen's New Year's Honours list. This award was for her work for the BBC.

50 years ago . . .

On 4 January 1972, Rose Heilbron became the first female judge to sit at the Central Criminal Court (known as the 'Old Bailey') in London.

75 years ago . . .

On 8 January 1947, the musician David Bowie was born. His first hit in the UK was 'Space Oddity' in 1969. The BBC played it while showing film footage of men landing on the moon.

*"January brings the snow,
Makes our feet and fingers glow."*

SARA COLERIDGE (1802–1852)

January can be a dull and dreary month after the excitement of Christmas and New Year's Eve – unless it snows of course! Who doesn't love a 'snow day'? Even if it doesn't snow, there are still lots of lovely things you can do, both outdoors and indoors, this month. You could wrap up warm and go for a walk to see what you can find. Yes, the trees are bare, but you should still be able to spot birds and other creatures out in the park or garden. There are also some wonderful festivals this month which offer a good excuse for getting friends round or throwing a party. So maybe January is not so dull after all!

Why is January Called January?

The calendar we use today was invented by the Romans. January was named after the Roman god Janus, who was the god of gates and doorways. He was always drawn with two faces looking in opposite directions – one face looked back at the year that had passed, and the other looked forwards into the new year.

DID YOU KNOW...

The temperature in January in the Northern Hemisphere is about the same as the temperature in July in the Southern Hemisphere.

New Year's Resolutions

On 31st December we often talk about 'making resolutions' for the new year. Why do we do this?

The tradition of making resolutions started with the Romans, too. Because the January god, Janus, was looking backwards and forwards at the same time, he became a symbol for the Romans of forgetting what had happened in the past and moving on into the future. January therefore became known as a month in which to forgive people and be kind.

Nowadays, people seem to worry more about getting fit and not eating chocolate – maybe we should be more like the Romans and make resolutions to be kinder instead?

Here are some ideas for resolutions that you might manage to keep . . .

- Look out for someone at school who needs a friend.
- Have a cake sale or organise a sponsored silence or a sponsored walk for charity.
- Clear out your old toys and clothes and take them to a charity shop. (Check with an adult before you give these things away!)
- Help out around the house and/or garden, if you have one.

FESTIVAL FUN

The colourful festivals of light such as Christmas, Hanukkah and Diwali might be over, but January has its fair share of celebrations to look forward to.

5th January *Twelfth Night*

For Christians, Twelfth Night used to be the day when Christmas was celebrated. In some countries, 5th January is still the day on which children get their presents.

It is also known as Epiphany, St Nicholas's Day and the Feast of the Three Kings. For most people in Britain, it's when the Christmas decorations come down, so it's not such a fun day.

5th January *Wassailing*

Wassailing is a pagan tradition. The word *wassail* comes from the Anglo-Saxon words *waes hael* which mean 'good health'. The festival is like many other winter celebrations in that it looks forward to what people hope for in the new year to come: good weather, good health and a good harvest.

Wassailing involves going out into the countryside to bless the apple trees. The wassail king and queen lead everyone in a sing-song around the tree to encourage it to produce lots of apples.

The wassail queen sometimes climbs the tree and offers it some bread soaked in cider. You could make mulled apple juice to soak bread in instead.

13th January *Lohri*

Hindus and Sikhs all over the world celebrate Lohri. During Lohri songs are sung to the sun god, Surya, thanking him for his warmth and praying for his return after the cold weather.

People drink *gurh* – a delicious sugary drink made from sugarcane. *Gajak* is also eaten – a thin, dry sweet made from roasted sesame seeds cooked in sugar syrup and spices. Children go from house to house singing folk songs and are given sweets. In the evening, a bonfire is lit and people gather together to dance.

17th January *Tu B'Shevat*

Tu B'Shevat is also known as Rosh Hashanah La'llanot, or 'The New Year of the Trees'. Like Wassailing, it is a time to give thanks for the trees coming to life and growing new green shoots after the winter. The day is celebrated with a feast of seven foods which are found growing in Israel: wheat, barley, grapes, figs, pomegranates, olives and dates.

25th January *Burns Night*

Burns Night celebrates the birthday of Scotland's most famous poet, Robert Burns. He wrote the song 'Auld Lang Syne', which we sing on New Year's Eve. In Scotland, people have a Burns Night supper, which includes the national dish of haggis, neeps (mashed turnips) and tatties (mashed potatoes).

OUTDOOR ADVENTURES

Just as the festivals remind us that January is a month of hope and looking forward to new things, nature is doing its best to give us hope, too. If you go out into the garden, the park or the woods near where you live, you will see signs of new life even on the darkest day. It depends on which area of the country you are in, of course. In the colder northern regions, plants take longer to appear, while down in the south you might see daffodils as early as 1st January.

One of the first plants that starts to peep up out of the ground this month is the snowdrop. These tiny white and green flowers might look fragile, but they can survive during the coldest weather – even with snow and ice!

Other plants are growing, too: have a look at the trees next time you go on a walk. Can you see any hazel catkins? They grow long before there are any leaves on the trees.

And then there are all the animals and birds to look out for. Squirrels are about, trying to remember where they buried nuts and seeds in the autumn! Have a look for birds building their nests, too – it may seem early, but blue tits and coal tits are very busy collecting twigs and feathers and fur for their nests. If you do find a nest, don't touch it even if it looks old – birds will not come back and lay their eggs there if a human has disturbed it.

Make a *Nature Notebook*

1. *Take some sheets of scrap paper, fold them in half to make a booklet, then staple them together where you've made the fold.*

2. *Remember to make the notebook small enough to fit into a pocket so that you can take it with you wherever you go.*

3. *Tie a piece of string to a pencil and stick the loose end of the string into the notebook with sticky tape or make a hole in the pages and thread the string through. Use the pencil to note down where and when you see things while you are out and about.*

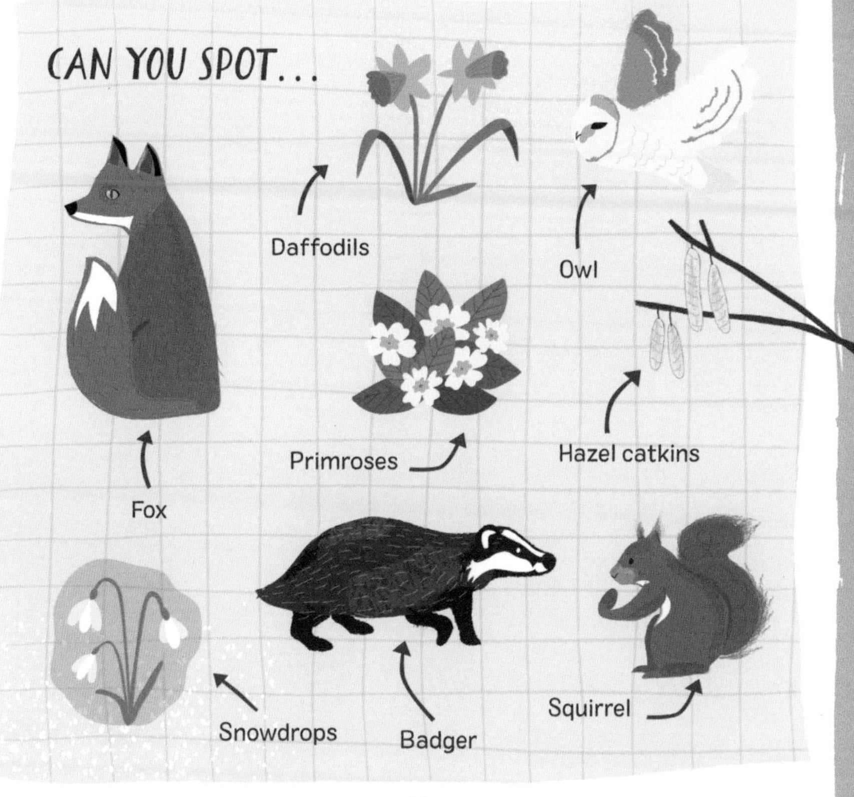

THE NIGHT SKY

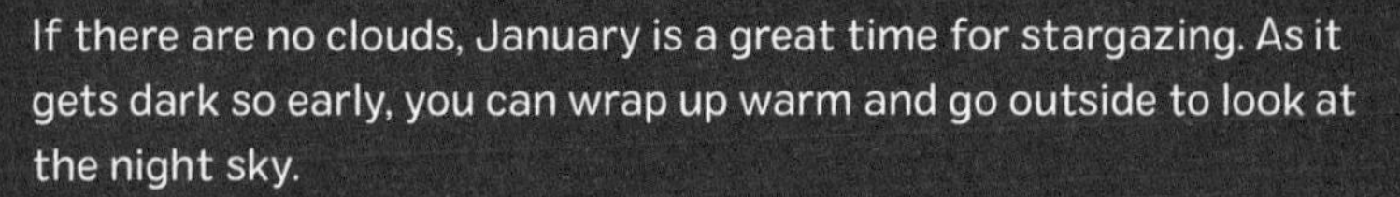

If there are no clouds, January is a great time for stargazing. As it gets dark so early, you can wrap up warm and go outside to look at the night sky.

Sometimes we see only part of the moon, depending on where the moon is in its journey across the sky. The different stages of this journey are called the 'phases of the moon'.

Phases of the Moon **in January 2022**

New Moon
2nd January

First Quarter
9th January

Full Moon
17th January

Last Quarter
25th January

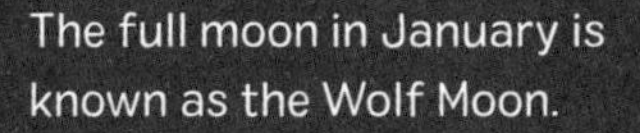

The full moon in January is known as the Wolf Moon.

BIRD SPOTTING

The RSPB holds a survey called the Big Garden Birdwatch at the end of January every year. This is to encourage people to record the different types of birds that regularly visit our gardens and streets so that we can keep an eye on their habits and see how the weather has affected them. More than half a million people take part every year. Check the RSPB website to see how you can get involved. **www.rspb.org.uk**

CAN YOU SPOT...

THE SEASIDE IN WINTER

Maybe a trip to the seaside is not at the top of your list of things to do at this time of the year! It's true that it's too chilly to go for a swim or a paddle, as the sea temperature has dropped to between 6°C and 10°C. However, you can still have fun hunting for shells, pebbles, seaweed and fossils. And there are some beautiful seabirds and other creatures for you to spot. Common seals can be seen along the UK coastline, and in Scotland, Wales and Cornwall you might also see porpoises. Wherever you go, make sure you take your nature notebook with you so that you can write down or draw what you see!

Take a bucket and a net with you, too. The weather may not be good enough for you to sit about making sandcastles, but hopping between the rock pools will keep you warm. See how many different objects you can find. The winter storms bring in all sorts of treasures, from pretty shells to funny-shaped driftwood to sea-softened pieces of coloured glass. Have a competition with your friends and family – the person with the most items wins. If you're really lucky, you may even find some real buried treasure!

DID YOU KNOW...

Rock pools are also known as 'tide pools' because the water level in them changes with the tides.

WINTER SENSES

Sometimes it's very tempting to stay snuggled up at home in January, but it is amazing how much better we feel once we have been outside. One of the best places to go to is a forest or wood where there are evergreen trees. You could try using all five of your senses while you are on your winter walk:

1. **Sight** Look closely at the trees. Many conifer trees (such as pine, spruce and fir) grow in a spiral pattern. You can guess how old the tree is by counting the spirals, or 'whorls' because, after about two years, the tree will grow a new whorl of branches each year.

2. **Sound** Stop and listen to the wood or forest. If it's dry, you could even lie down on the ground for a bit. Can you hear the wind through the trees? Or the rustle of animals or birds? How does the ground sound when you walk on it?

3. **Touch** Have a look around you for pine cones or dried leaves. What do they feel like? Run your fingers over a tree trunk. Do you feel excited? Happy? Calm?

4. **Smell** Breathe in the smells around you. If you've walked here before, does the wood smell different to the last time you were here?

5. **Taste** We can't eat the actual trees, of course! But when we smell, we use our sense of taste as well. What can you taste from the air around you?

Recipe for *Lovely Lentils*

There is nothing like sitting down to a big bowl of warming winter soup – especially if you've just come in from a long, blustery walk in the woods! You'll need an adult to help with this recipe.

You will need:

Sharp knife
Chopping board
Large saucepan with lid
Wooden spoon
Garlic press
Kettle
Measuring jug

1 large white onion
1 carrot
2 sticks celery
1 tablespoon of cooking oil
1 teaspoon of ground cumin or curry powder (optional)
Garlic clove
500 g dried red lentils
1 l boiling water
Vegetable stock cubes or powder (to make 1 l)
1 tin chopped tomatoes
Salt and pepper
½ tin coconut milk (optional)
1 packet washed spinach (optional)
Full-fat Greek yoghurt (optional)

1. *Ask an adult to help you chop the onion, carrot and celery into small chunks.*
2. *Pour the oil into the saucepan and warm over a medium heat on the stove.*
3. *Carefully tip the chopped vegetables into the pan and stir with the wooden spoon. Add the cumin or curry powder if you like a spicy flavour.*
4. *Peel and crush the garlic, then add it to the saucepan and stir for about 5 minutes, until the vegetables are soft.*
5. *Add the lentils and stir until they are coated in the cooked vegetables.*
6. *Put the vegetable stock cubes or powder into the measuring jug. Boil the kettle, then carefully pour the boiling water into the jug. Stir and add the stock to the saucepan.*
7. *Put the lid on the saucepan and leave to simmer for about 20 minutes until the lentils have puffed up and look soft.*
8. *Add the tin of tomatoes, and ½ tin of coconut milk if you like, and stir until warmed through.*
9. *Add salt and pepper.*
10. *Pour into bowls and add a spoonful of Greek yoghurt and a handful of fresh spinach on top if you like. Serve with warm, crusty bread.*

FEBRUARY

SPECIAL DAYS

1st Chinese New Year (Year of the Tiger)

2nd Imbolc (pagan celebration)/ Candlemas (Christian festival)

14th St Valentine's Day

ANNIVERSARIES

70 years ago . . .

On 6 February 1952, Elizabeth II became the monarch after the death of her father, King George VI. She was the first queen of the UK and Commonwealth since Queen Victoria. She heard the news herself while staying in a treehouse at the Treetops Hotel in Kenya!

210 years ago . . .

On 7 February 1812, the writer Charles Dickens was born in Portsmouth. He is famous for many books including *Oliver Twist* and *A Christmas Carol*.

"Late February days;
and now at last, Might you have
thought that Winter's woe was passed."

WILLIAM MORRIS (1834–1896)

February is a short month – this year it has only 28 days. Many people think this is good, as the weather can be bad and the days are quite dark. In fact, the days are getting longer, and by the end of February we will have two hours more daylight.

Spring is not far away: animals and plants are slowly waking up as nature gets ready to show off all its colours and lovely smells. Look around – what plants can you see peeking out of the soil? There will be green shoots out there, however small.

Many religions think of February as a quiet month in which to be still and thankful. Some hold 'fasts', which means that they do not eat during the day to help them concentrate on prayer and mindfulness. Why not try having some quiet time each day in February? It's a good way to feel grateful for things in life – especially on a cold, dark day!

Why is February Called February?

The Latin name for this month was *Februarius*. It came from the Latin word *februum* which means 'purification'. The Romans thought of the fifth day of this month as the official first day of spring. On the fifteenth they celebrated a festival called *Februa*.

This was a time to get rid of evil spirits and to cleanse the air so that people felt fit and healthy for spring. This is where we get our idea of spring cleaning from. Perhaps you could use the colder, darker days this month to tidy your bedroom or help clear out the shed or garage.

February Birth Signs

Aquarius The sign of the water-carrier. Some people believe that if you have your birthday between 20th January and 18th February, then this is your sign. You are supposed to be an inquisitive and logical person.

Pisces The sign of the fish. If you were born between 19th February and 20th March, then you are a Piscean. Some people believe this means you are creative and good at working things out based on your feelings.

It Was a Dark and Snowy Night . . .

On 8 February 1885, in Devon in the south of England, a great unexplained mystery happened. Villagers up and down the Exe river were all huddled indoors, keeping close to their fires and trying to stay warm. No one was out in the streets or the fields. The snow came down thick and soft and settled all over everything. It was eerily quiet. Everyone went to bed, safe and sound. The next morning, on opening their shutters, people saw the strangest sight: hundreds upon hundreds of bizarre footprints could be seen in the snow, going on for about 160 kilometres. They were shaped like the hoof of a cow, sheep or goat, except that no normal animal could have made the marks, because it looked like the creature had only one leg – all the footprints were in a single line. The story was reported in the newspapers at the time. No one has ever been able to explain where the hoof marks came from. Spooky!

FESTIVAL FUN

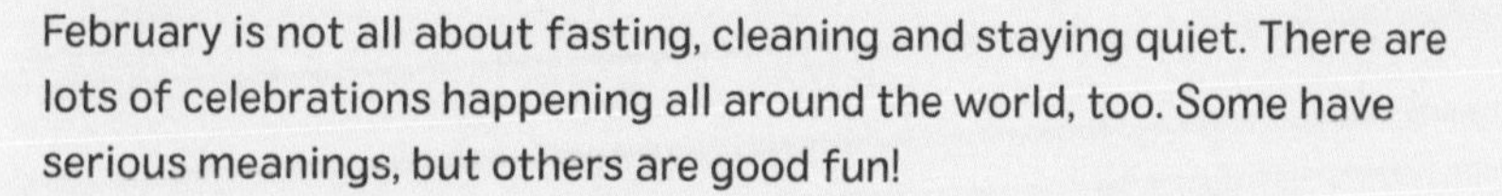

February is not all about fasting, cleaning and staying quiet. There are lots of celebrations happening all around the world, too. Some have serious meanings, but others are good fun!

1st February *Chinese New Year*

Chinese New Year is a noisy and colourful occasion and there will be festivities in big cities throughout the UK. There are firecrackers, lion and dragon dances, music, parades, lanterns and special foods such as noodles. People wear red clothes for luck and to ward off evil spirits.

2022 is the Year of the Tiger. In Chinese culture, the tiger is believed to be the protector of children. Babies and toddlers often wear clothes with tiger designs on them for good luck. People born in the Year of the Tiger are said to be brave and active people who enjoy challenges and adventures.

Recipe for *Sesame Noodles*

Serves 4. You can add other things to this recipe such as cooked chicken and cooked prawns if you like.

You will need:

Whisk	**4 tablespoons of dark soy sauce**
Small bowl	**2 garlic cloves, finely sliced or crushed**
Saucepan	**2 tablespoons of rice vinegar**
Sieve	**3 tablespoons of sesame oil**
Chopsticks	**Splash of chilli oil or a pinch of dried red chillies**
	300 g thin dried egg noodles
	4 spring onions (scallions), finely sliced

1 *Whisk together the soy sauce, garlic, rice vinegar and oils.*

2 *Prepare the egg noodles following the instructions on the packet.*

3 *Pour the sauce over the warm noodles, top with spring onions and eat straight away!*

If you are not used to using chopsticks, have a go:

Step 1:

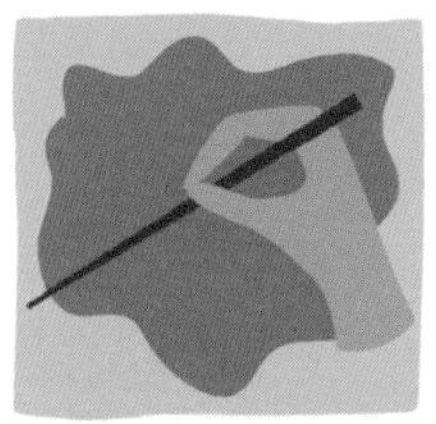

Hold the upper chopstick like a pencil, about one-third of the way from the top.

Step 2:

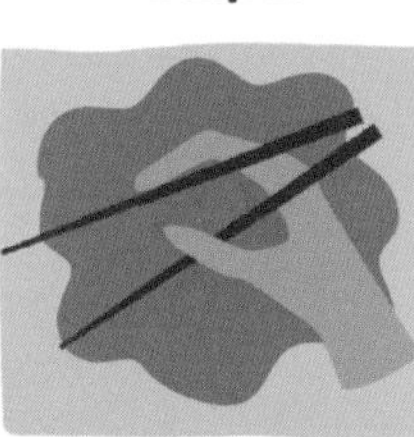

Place the second chopstick against your fourth finger and hold it in place with your thumb.

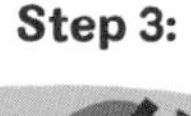

Step 3:

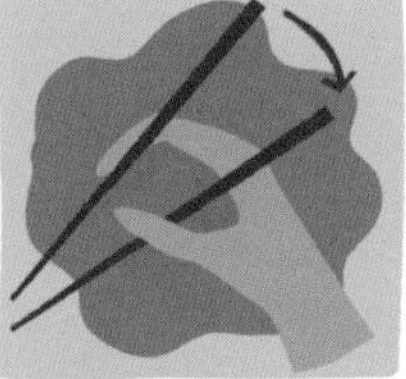

Move the upper chopstick with your thumb, first and middle fingers.

2nd February *Imbolc*

Imbolc (pronounced 'imulk') is a pagan festival. Its name comes from the Celtic word *imbolg* which means 'in the belly'. This is because nature seems to be expecting lots of babies at this time of year – baby animals, baby trees, baby flowers and fruit and vegetables. Everything is hidden away at the moment, but that doesn't mean nothing is happening deep in the cold, dark ground – or inside pregnant animals! To celebrate, people sometimes make dolls from corn called 'Bridey dolls' which are said to bring good luck.

2nd February *Candlemas*

Candlemas is a Christian festival. It celebrates the day that the baby Jesus was taken to the temple for the first time. The festival always takes place on 2nd February and marks the end of the Christmas season. At Ripon Cathedral in Yorkshire, people celebrate by lighting 5,000 candles to symbolise Jesus bringing light into the darkness of the world.

14th February *St Valentine's Day*

St Valentine's Day is an ancient tradition. Today, it's seen as a day to celebrate love. People send cards and flowers (particularly red roses), chocolates and other gifts. In some parts of Norfolk and Suffolk there is an old custom of leaving presents on people's doorsteps on St Valentine's Eve, the night before St Valentine's Day.

Recipe for *Heart-shaped Biscuits*

What better way to show your love for someone than by making these delicious biscuits? (Hopefully they'll share them with you, too!)

You will need:

Baking tray
Greaseproof paper
Large bowl
Electric hand whisk
Sieve
Wooden spoon
Rolling pin
Heart-shaped biscuit cutters (different sizes if possible)
Small blunt knife
Wire rack

150 g butter (softened)
100 g caster sugar
1 large egg
250 g plain flour plus extra for dusting
1 teaspoon of baking powder
1 pinch salt
1 teaspoon of vanilla extract
150 g icing sugar, sieved
Red or pink food colouring
Sugar sprinkles

1. *Preheat the oven to 180°C/ 160°C fan/Gas Mark 4 and line a baking tray with greaseproof paper.*
2. *In the large bowl, whisk together the butter and sugar. When the mixture looks light and creamy, add the egg and mix thoroughly.*
3. *Sieve the flour, baking powder and salt into the mixture.*
4. *Add the vanilla extract and mix with the wooden spoon until the mixture looks like dough.*
5. *Place the dough on a work surface sprinkled with flour and roll to about 1 cm thickness.*
6. *Use the cutters to cut out hearts and place them on to the lined baking tray (you may need more than one tray, or to cook in batches).*
7. *Bake for 8–12 minutes, until the hearts are lightly golden around the edges.*
8. *Put them on the wire rack to cool while you make the icing.*
9. *Make the icing following the instructions on the packet and add food colouring until you get the shade of red or pink that you want. Save some white icing if you want some white hearts.*
10. *Spread the icing on to the biscuits with the small, blunt knife and sprinkle on the decorations.*
11. *Serve once the icing has set. Or put them in a pretty box and give as a gift.*

SNOW IS FALLING

Christmas cards often have snowy scenes on them, but actually we hardly ever have snow in December in Britain. It is more likely that you will see snow in February. There's nothing like wrapping up warm and running outside to make footprints in the freshly fallen snow.

If you're lucky enough to get lots of snow, you could build a snow castle. Make sure you are wearing warm clothes and waterproof gloves. Make your castle in the same way that you would make a sandcastle – you can pack mounds of snow together with your hands or if you have buckets and spades left over from your summer holiday, you could use them! Make lots of 'turrets' using the buckets or mounds and then join them together with low snow 'walls'. You could make flags with sticks and pieces of paper or strips of old cloth, which you could decorate. Or you could look for stones or interestingly shaped twigs to make patterns on the walls and turrets of your castle.

WEATHER

*"When halo rings moon or Sun,
Rain's approaching on the run."*

This is an old country saying, and there is some truth in it. If you see a halo around the moon or sun at this time of year, it is because ice crystals can sometimes form in high clouds. These make a ring or 'halo' appear, and later these crystals may fall as rain. Rainy days can seem boring, but remember that the rain is doing a good job of watering all those tiny plants that are waiting for spring to arrive. Also, the rain comes from clouds which come in all shapes and sizes. Cloud spotting can be fun – what kind of pictures and shapes can you see in the clouds today?

Cloud Spotting

Most of our names for clouds come from Latin. They are a combination of the following:

Stratus/strato =
low, flat/layered and smooth

Cumulus/cumulo =
heaped up/puffy, like cauliflower

Cirrus/cirro =
high up/wispy

Alto =
medium level

Nimbus/nimbo =
rain-bearing cloud

Combining the names tells you a bit more about the clouds. For example: nimbus + stratus = 'nimbostratus'. This is a cloud which is flat and layered and will probably bring rain. 'Cumulonimbus' is a puffy cloud which will bring rain, too.

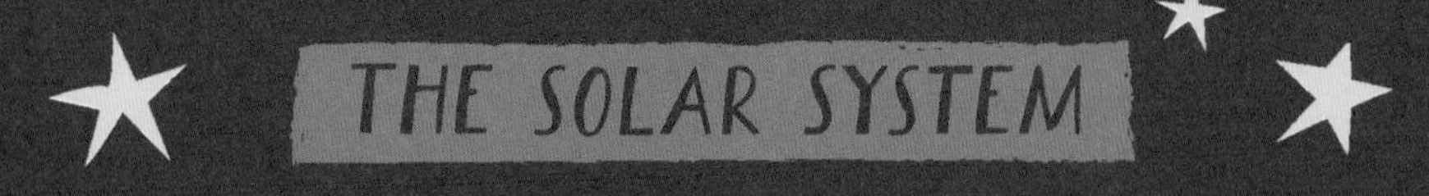

THE SOLAR SYSTEM

The sun is in the middle of the solar system – the Earth and all the planets listed below move around the sun, and the moon moves around the Earth.

Constellation of the Month

Canis Major, or the 'Great Dog', can be seen this month. It chases Orion, the 'Hunter', across the sky. To find it, look for Sirius, the 'Dog Star'. In fact, this is two stars very close together which is why it is so bright. It is one of the closest stars to Planet Earth.

DID YOU KNOW...

The full moon in February was known by Native American tribes as the Snow Moon because the heaviest snows often fell in February.

WILDLIFE ON THE MOVE

Toads, frogs and newts are often on the move in February. They walk and hop a long way back to their ponds to find others to breed with. This sometimes gets them into trouble, as they have to cross roads between their winter homes and their ponds.

To help prevent the amphibians from getting squashed, there are Toad Patrols up and down the country which go out in the evenings and pick the creatures up and carry them safely across the road. You can help amphibians to migrate safely by joining a patrol near you.

To find a Toad Crossing near you, go to **www.froglife.org** and follow the links. It's good fun and you can do some stargazing and wildlife-watching, too, as foxes, badgers and owls are out in the evening as well.

CAN YOU SPOT...

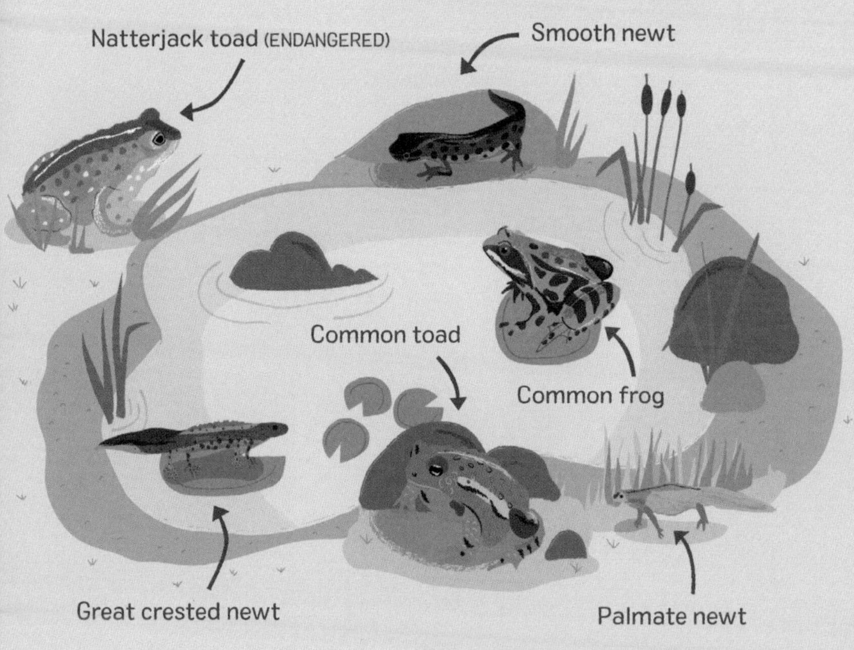

FEED THE BIRDS

Small birds are hungry at this time of year. They need to eat all day to get enough food to keep them going through the winter. You can help by making your own treats for the birds using food scraps from home.

You don't need to spend a lot of money on fancy feeders or a beautiful bird table. You'll need to buy the bird seed and nuts, but if you buy a big sack from a garden centre it is cheaper than buying small quantities, and it will last a long time. You can also use a surprising amount of food scraps that are easy to find at home. Raisins, sultanas, other dried fruit or unsalted nuts go down well with any wild bird.

Make an *Orange Bird Feeder*

These are very easy and fun to make. And the best thing is, you can make yourself a tasty treat, too! Ask an adult to help you cut the oranges in half and then use a juicer or squeezer to make some delicious fresh orange juice. Put it in the fridge and enjoy it as a reward once you have finished making these pretty feeders.

You will need:

Shallow oven dish
Wooden spoon
Empty orange halves
Saucepan
Bird seeds
Raisins
Unsalted nuts
Unsalted nut butter or dairy butter or lard

1 *Pour the seeds, fruit and/or nuts into the dish and give them a good stir with the wooden spoon.*

2 *Scoop up a handful of the bird food and press it into the orange halves.*

3 *Ask an adult to help you melt the fat or spread you have chosen to use.*

4 *Pour the melted fat or spread into the orange cups.*

5 *Use the wooden spoon to gently pat the mixture down into the orange cups. Let it solidify.*

6 *Put them on the bird table or windowsill.*

MARCH

SPECIAL DAYS

1st Shrove Tuesday (Pancake Day)/ Isra and Mi'raj (Muslim celebration)/St David's Day (Wales)

2nd Ash Wednesday (Christian festival)

5th St Piran's Day (Cornwall)

17th Purim (Jewish festival)/St Patrick's Day (Ireland)

18th Holi (Hindu festival of colours)

20th Spring equinox (first day of spring)/Ostara (pagan celebration)

27th Mother's Day/Daylight saving (clocks go forward)

ANNIVERSARIES

75 years ago . . .

On 25 March 1947, the British musician Elton John was born. He is famous for songs such as 'Tiny Dancer' and 'Rocket Man'. In 2019, a film called *Rocketman* was made about his life and work.

175 years ago . . .

On 3 March 1847, the inventor Alexander Graham Bell was born in Edinburgh, Scotland. He is famous for inventing the telephone.

"It was one of those March days when the sun shines hot and the wind blows cold."

CHARLES DICKENS (1812–1870)

This quote describes very well how we might look out of the window in March and think, "It looks lovely out there!" only to go outside and find ourselves shivering our socks off! At least the days are getting longer though.

DID YOU KNOW...

'March' comes from the Roman word *Martius*. The month was named after the god of war and farming. That might seem a strange combination, but both war and farming began again in March after the long winter months. Even soldiers didn't like getting cold and wet!

Phases of the Moon in March 2022

New Moon	First Quarter	Full Moon	Last Quarter
2nd March	10th March	18th March	25th March

Spring Equinox

20th March is the spring equinox. This is one of the days in the year in which the number of hours of daylight is exactly equal to the number of hours of darkness. This happens because the rays of the sun are shining straight at the equator (the middle of the Earth).

Constellation of the Month

Ursa Major can be seen to the north at this time of year. Its name is Latin for 'Great Bear'. The Romans had a story that a beautiful woman called Callisto was transformed into a bear by the goddess Artemis and thrown up into the stars. The seven brightest stars of this constellation form a saucepan shape often known as the 'Plough' or the 'Big Dipper'.

FESTIVAL FUN

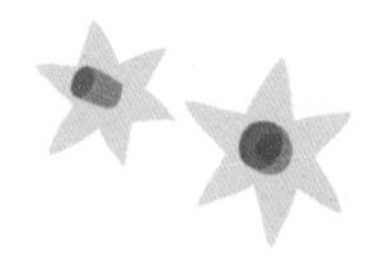

1st March *Shrove Tuesday (Pancake Day)*

Shrove Tuesday gets its name from the ancient Christian practice of being 'shriven', which means being forgiven for things you've done wrong. It was traditional to tell a priest about anything bad you had done to get it out of the way before Lent, the season of fasting. Then, during the fast, you could concentrate on asking for forgiveness and promising to live a better life. On Shrove Tuesday, people used up eggs and fatty foods because during Lent they were not allowed to eat these things. One of the best ways of using up eggs and fat is to make pancakes, and a lot of people still do this today. That is why we also call this day Pancake Day.

1st March *Isra and Mi'raj*

This festival is in two parts. The first part, the *Isra* or the 'Night Journey', starts on the evening before the day of celebrations. Muslims remember the Prophet Muhammad's journey from Mecca to Jerusalem and then to heaven. Muslim people believe the Night Journey started when the Angel Gabriel took the Prophet Muhammad to Jerusalem on a winged horse, where he met and prayed with prophets including Moses and Jesus.

The second part is the *Mi'raj*, which means 'ladder' in Arabic. This was when the Prophet Muhammad was carried up to heaven by Gabriel where he spoke to Allah (God), who told the Prophet that Muslims should say their prayers five times a day. At Isra and Mi'raj, Muslim people say prayers during the night and Muslim cities keep their lights on all night.

18th March *Holi*

Holi is a Hindu festival also known as the 'festival of colours' or the 'festival of love', when Hindus celebrate the victory of good over evil and the arrival of spring. They meet to play and laugh, forget and forgive, and make up with people they have fallen out with! Holi lasts for a night and a day, starting on the evening of the Purnima (full moon day). People light bonfires and pray that evil will be destroyed. Then they smear each other with coloured paints and drench each other using water pistols and water-filled balloons!

20th March *Ostara*

Ostara is a pagan festival which is celebrated at the spring equinox. For pagans, it's a time of year when everything in the natural world is in perfect balance because the day and the night are the same length. The festival takes its name from Ostara or Ēostre, the goddess of renewal and rebirth, who has the head of a hare.

27th March *Mother's Day*

Mother's Day (or Mothering Sunday) always falls on the fourth Sunday in Lent, three weeks before Easter Day. It was originally a Christian festival, and it has now become a day for people to say thank you to their mothers or carers. Why not make a card or promise jar (p. 40) to show your mother or carer how much they mean to you?

SHOW A LITTLE LOVE

Mother's Day is a very old festival. People celebrated it in ancient Greece when the mother goddess, Rhea, was worshipped. Later, Christians celebrated the day as a time for people to go back to their 'mother' church if they had moved away from their home town. Nowadays, we spend the day saying thank you to our mothers or carers or special female relatives or friends with a card, gift or meal.

Make a *Mother's Day Promise Jar*

You will need:

Scraps of paper – white or coloured
Scissors or pinking shears
Pen or pencil
Clean old jam jar – decorated with stickers or glitter glue pens if you like
Colourful recycled wrapping paper or pages from a magazine
Elastic band
Length of thin ribbon

TOP TIP

Why not make a lovely breakfast and lay the table – maybe with a vase of flowers, too? Then leave the jar of promises out as a surprise as well!

1. *Cut your scraps of paper into squares that are about 6 cm x 6 cm, using the scissors or pinking shears.*
2. *Write a promise on each piece of paper. Ten is probably enough. Some ideas are: "I will make you a cup of tea." "I will walk the dog."*
3. *Fold each piece of paper in half and put them in the jar.*
4. *Put the lid, top down, on the sheet of wrapping paper or a page from a magazine and draw a larger circle around it. You can do this by hand – don't worry if it's not a perfect circle.*
5. *Cut out the large circle with the scissors or pinking shears.*
6. *Screw the lid on to the jar and place the large paper circle on top.*
7. *Fix it in place with the elastic band and tie some ribbon over the band.*

Recipe for *Butterfly Cakes*

Say a big thank you to your mother or carer with these butterfly cakes.

You will need:

12-bun muffin tin
12 muffin cases
Food processor
Sieve
Large metal spoon
Spatula
Metal skewer
Wire rack
Small mixing bowl
Sharp knife

125 g unsalted butter, softened
125 g caster sugar
2 large eggs
½ teaspoon of vanilla extract
125 g self-raising flour
1 heaped teaspoon of baking powder
2–3 tablespoons of milk
100 g very soft unsalted butter (for the icing)
100 g icing sugar, sieved
Food colouring and flower or butterfly sprinkles

1. *Heat the oven to 200°C/180°C fan/Gas Mark 6. Pop the muffin cases into the tin.*
2. *Put the butter, sugar, eggs, vanilla extract, flour and baking powder into the food processor.*
3. *Mix gently, carefully adding the milk until you have a soft mixture.*
4. *Divide the mixture between the muffin cases using the large metal spoon and spatula.*
5. *Bake for 15–20 minutes until the tops of the cakes have risen like mini mountains. Insert the metal skewer into the cakes to check they are cooked – it should come out clean.*
6. *Leave your cakes for 10 minutes, then place them on a wire rack to cool.*
7. *Meanwhile, make the butter icing. Use the food processor again to beat very soft butter until smooth.*
8. *Slowly add the sieved icing sugar to the butter while mixing. Add food colouring if you like.*
9. *Ask an adult to help you slice off the 'mountain' part of each cake and carefully cut each part in half – these will be your butterfly 'wings'.*
10. *Put a blob of butter icing on to the flat top of each cake and then stick the wings in.*
11. *Add flower or butterfly sprinkles. Serve and enjoy with your mother or carer!*

MARCH MADNESS!

Did you know that in March hares start to behave in a strange way? If you are lucky enough to spot any, you'll probably see them leaping about crazily.

You might even find them standing on their back legs and boxing each other with their fists! This behaviour seems so weird that we sometimes use the expression "mad as a March hare" to describe a human who is acting in a bizarre way.

Actually, there is a very good reason why hares act like this in March: the male hares are looking for females to mate with at this time of year. The hares box and chase each other as they try to find mates.

OUT AND ABOUT

There are more birds and animals to see in March. Some of them, such as chiffchaffs and wheatears, are visitors from other countries. It will depend where you live in the UK as to whether you are likely to see these birds. Some of them are found only in wetland areas or by the sea.

CAN YOU SPOT...

Chiffchaff

Sand martin

Sandwich tern

Blackcap

Chaffinch

Wheatear

Skylark

Lapwing

DID YOU KNOW...

Skylarks start singing before the sun rises, so their voice is one of the first to be heard in the dawn chorus. Sadly, the numbers of skylarks are falling in all European countries. It is thought that this is because crops are now sown in autumn rather than in spring – this means that skylarks no longer have the habitat they need in which to breed and survive.

GET WET

Building a dam is a great outdoors activity now that spring is on its way. You'll need to ask an adult to help you find the best place to build your dam. And make sure everyone wears wellies and some waterproof clothing!

First choose a narrow stream of clean, shallow water where you can paddle safely. Then you need to start looking for driftwood, loose mud, rocks and pebbles. You'll use these to build the dam. You'll find the best bits and pieces at places where the stream bends, as rocks and things will tend to get stuck there.

See if you can stop the stream from flowing or change its direction by building up your dam. Where does the water go?

Don't forget to take down your dam before you go home so that the stream can flow freely again.

DID YOU KNOW...

Beavers create dams to make a pond of deep, quiet water. They use their sharp teeth and strong jaws to bite through the trunks of trees. The trees fall into the water to make a sort of pond. Then the beavers chew off branches and sticks to make islands of wood in the pond in order to build their homes or 'lodges'.

DOWN BY THE RIVER

If you can get to a river, keep a sharp lookout for kingfishers. At this time of year the male bird is very busy, zipping along the surface of the water looking for fish.

TOP TIP

Note down what you find in your nature notebook!

CAN YOU SPOT...

Frog

Frog spawn

Tadpoles

Pond snail

Whirligig beetle

Backswimmer

Pond skater

Dragonfly nymph

Newt

GET PLANTING!

Now is the perfect time to start planting things. And it's a great idea to plant something that grows pretty quickly because then you don't have to wait too long to see the results. A bean will sprout within one to two weeks. If you take care of it and plant it out carefully, you'll have a whole beanstalk full of delicious beans by the summer. Activities that you can eat are always the best!

Grow a *Bean in a Jar*

You don't need a veg patch or allotment for this activity - put the jar on a windowsill and then plant out into a pot.

You will need:

Clean, empty jam jar
Kitchen roll
1 broad bean seed or 1 dried butter bean from the supermarket
Water
10 cm plant pot
Compost

1. *Rinse the jam jar and leave it a little damp inside.*
2. *Put a folded piece of kitchen roll into the jar and press it up against the glass.*
3. *Pop the bean seed in between the kitchen roll and the glass and leave the jar on the windowsill.*
4. *Add a spoonful of water to the seed every day – just enough to keep the jar moist but not waterlogged.*
5. *Check the bean after a few days and you should notice that it will have sprouted.*
6. *After a couple of weeks, you'll have your own broad bean seedling! You'll be able to plant it out into the 10 cm plant pot of compost.*
7. *If you have space outside, you can plant your seedling in the ground.*

TOP TIP

As your plant gets larger, you will need to support it with a lolly stick or twig. When it's about 75 cm high, snip off the top and wait for your bean harvest!

APRIL

SPECIAL DAYS

1st April Fool's Day

2nd Ramadan begins (Muslim month of prayer and fasting)

15th Pesach (Jewish celebration) begins

17th Easter Sunday (Christian celebration)

22nd Earth Day

23rd St George's Day (England)/William Shakespeare's birthday

ANNIVERSARIES

30 years ago . . .

On 27 April 1992 Betty Boothroyd became the first woman in the 700-year history of the British House of Commons to be elected Speaker.

150 years ago . . .

On 2 April 1872, the American inventor Samuel Morse died. He is famous for inventing the Morse Code, which uses dots and dashes to represent letters and numbers.

"The sun was warm but the wind was chill. You know how it is with an April Day"

ROBERT FROST (1874–1963)

The weather can be so confusing in April, as the quote above suggests: you might look out of the window and see bright sunshine, but when you go outside it might be freezing cold! And then there are those April showers that seem to come without warning, too. Still, without that rain, we wouldn't see the gorgeous blossom and green shoots that start to come out at this time of year.

The mornings are often very cold in April. Sometimes there are still sharp frosts overnight and you might see white feathers of ice crystals on the grass when you wake up. If you live in the hills, you might also get snow.

But then on other days, there will be a bright burst of hot spring weather and you'll feel like running around in a T-shirt and shorts! Basically, the best advice to follow is to be prepared for all weathers – so don't forget to take an umbrella and a jumper out with you this month, even if the sun is shining when you leave the house!

Do you know the difference between a new moon, a full moon and a blue moon?

A **new moon** is a moon we cannot see from Earth! This is because the moon is between the Earth and the sun and therefore is not lit up.

A **full moon** is when the complete circle of the moon can be seen in the sky. The full moon in April is called the Pink Moon.

A **blue moon** happens when there are two full moons in the same month. The last blue moon was on 31 October 2020, and the next one will be on 31 August 2023. This is because the moon goes through all of its phases in 28 days, whereas our months can be 28, 29, 30 or 31 days long. So every two or three years, there will be a month or two in the year when there are two full moons.

DID YOU KNOW...

The first Sunday in April is called 'Daffodil Day'. In Victorian times people used to pick daffodils to give to the sick. Nowadays the daffodil is used as a symbol by the charity Marie Curie in their fundraising appeals.

FESTIVAL FUN

1st April *April Fool's Day*

April Fool's Day is celebrated by people playing tricks on one another. Sometimes there are even April Fool's Day stories on the news. One of the most famous of these was in 1957 on the BBC television programme *Panorama*. The programme reported that in Italy there were spaghetti trees! Lots of people believed this because in 1957 not many people in Britain had eaten spaghetti, so they didn't know that it was made from flour and water and it definitely did not grow on trees . . .

DID YOU KNOW . . .

There are a few unofficial rules about April Fool's Day tricks. The first is to do no harm – after all, the aim is to make someone look and feel silly. The second is that you can only play tricks before midday. If you try to trick someone in the afternoon, you become the fool!

2nd April *Ramadan Begins*

The month of Ramadan traditionally begins after the new moon, so the date for Ramadan changes from year to year. During Ramadan, Muslims hold a fast during the hours of daylight, which means they are not allowed to eat or drink from the moment the sun comes up until the moment it sets. People must also try not to gossip or fight during Ramadan. Muslims use the daylight hours to focus on saying prayers and giving money and possessions to charity. Some people try to learn the whole holy book, the *Qur'an*, during this time!

15th April *Pesach*

Jewish people celebrate Pesach to remember how Moses helped the Israelites escape from Egypt to a new life in the Promised Land.

Recipe for *Pesach Apple Cake*

At Pesach, Jewish people are not allowed to mix dairy with meat or eggs, so you can't make a cake with butter and eggs. But this recipe uses other ingredients and the results are just as tasty!

You will need:

23 cm springform cake tin or Bundt cake mould
Food processor
Peeler
Grater
Kitchen roll
Large bowl
Spatula
Metal skewer
Wire rack

Oil for greasing
Icing sugar for dusting
6 large eggs
200 g caster sugar
4 green eating apples
300 g almond flour
40 g potato flour

1. *Heat the oven to 170°C/ 150°C fan/ Gas Mark 3.*
2. *Lightly oil the cake tin or mould and dust with icing sugar.*
3. *Crack the eggs into the food processor and add the caster sugar. Whisk for about 10 minutes until the mixture is light and fluffy.*
4. *Meanwhile, ask an adult to help you to peel and grate the apples.*
5. *Tear off 4 sheets of kitchen roll and place the grated apple in the middle. Parcel it up and, over the large bowl, squeeze the grated apple to remove the juice.*
6. *Set the mixer to a low speed, then add the almond and potato flours and mix well.*
7. *Use the spatula to gently fold in the grated apple and pour the mixture into the tin or mould.*
8. *Bake the cake for 60–70 minutes. A metal skewer inserted into the centre of the cake should come out clean.*
9. *Leave the cake to cool in the tin or mould on a wire rack for 10 minutes. Then flip the cake out on to a serving plate, dust with icing sugar and enjoy!*

FESTIVAL FUN

17th April *Easter Sunday*

The Christian festival of Easter starts on the Thursday before Easter Sunday with a day called 'Maundy Thursday', when Christians believe that Jesus invited his followers to a meal called the 'Last Supper'. Easter ends on Easter Sunday, when Christians believe that Jesus came back from the dead. It is a time for new life and rebirth. Easter eggs are also popular on this day.

Some people believe that the tradition of giving and receiving Easter eggs comes from the pagan festival Ostara, or Ēostre. The Easter Bunny, who is supposed to bring the eggs, is thought to come from the pagan religion, which has the hare as the symbol of new life. Christians use the symbol of the Easter egg to represent rebirth and the resurrection of Jesus.

EGG-CELLENT ACTIVITIES

Today, a lot of people in Britain give and receive Easter eggs over Easter weekend, whether or not they celebrate any religious festivals.

The Hunt is On!

Easter egg hunts are always exciting. You could ask an adult to hide mini chocolate eggs outside in the garden or in an area of your local park, or even while you are out on a walk. Then see how quickly you can find them – and don't eat too many on the way!

Make an *Easter Suncatcher*

These pretty Easter suncatchers are easy to make and look beautiful hanging in the window.

You will need:

50 cm clear baking parchment
Newspaper
Tissue paper in different colours
Scissors
PVA glue
Black sugar paper or thin card
White pencil
Coloured ribbon or string

1. *Lie the clear baking parchment on a table covered with newspaper.*
2. *Carefully cut out lots of squares or triangles of the coloured tissue paper and glue them all over the baking parchment so that you have made a collage of colour. Leave to dry.*
3. *Take the black card or paper and draw some simple Easter shapes on each sheet with the white pencil. You could try an egg, a chick, a flower or a rabbit.*
4. *Cut out these shapes and then carefully cut out the centre of each one so that you make a black frame.*
5. *Stick each frame over the tissue collage. Once dry, cut around the outside of the frame.*
6. *Cut a length of ribbon or string to about 25 cm and form a loop, then glue the ends on to the back of the black frame.*
7. *They are now ready to hang in the window – watch the sunlight stream in and see what happens to the patterns it makes in your room!*

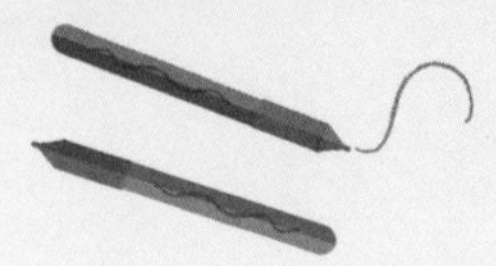

Make an *Egghead*

This is a fun indoor gardening activity – and you can eat the results! Use the larger part of any egg shells saved from after you've had boiled eggs or after you've used some eggs for baking.

You will need:

Empty eggshells
Empty egg box
Felt-tip pens
Cotton wool
Cress seeds

TOP TIP

If you don't want to make edible eggheads, you can use grass seed instead of cress. The grass will grow back so you can style your eggheads' hair again and again.

1 *Wash out the eggshells and sit them in the egg box.*

2 *Draw on some crazy faces with the felt-tip pens.*

3 *Put some cotton wool inside the shells and sprinkle some water on to make it damp.*

4 *Sprinkle lots of cress seeds all over the wet cotton wool – the more seeds you pour in, the more 'hair' your eggheads will grow!*

5 *Put the box of eggheads on a sunny windowsill and wait for the 'hair' to sprout.*

6 *Check the cotton wool each day and add a little water if the cotton wool feels dry when you touch it. Do not over-water the cress.*

7 *When the cress 'hair' has grown, you can give your eggheads a haircut! Use scissors to cut the cress and add it to chopped-up boiled eggs and mayonnaise for a tasty sandwich filling.*

8 *When you're finished with your eggheads, you can put them in the compost.*

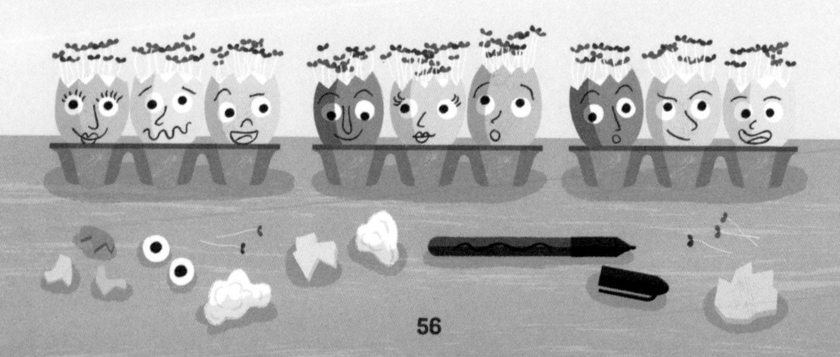

BE GREEN FOR EARTH DAY

22nd April is Earth Day. This is a day to focus on what we can do to help the environment and protect our planet. The first Earth Day was in 1970. It was set up by an American politician called Senator Gaylord Nelson because he thought it was important for children to be taught about the environment in school.

Here are some things you could do on Earth Day:

★ Walk or cycle to school instead of going by car or bus.
★ Turn off lights when you leave the room.
★ Turn off electrical appliances such as the TV, chargers and computer at the wall when you are not using them.
★ Try not to use a computer, tablet or the TV at all for just one day!
★ Get outside and find a green space to walk or play in – you don't have to have a garden or live in the country to do this. Find a square or a park and take time to look at the trees, plants, birds and insects.
★ If you have space at home, why not do some spring planting?
★ Ask your grown-ups if you can swap to more environmentally friendly cleaning products. Did you know that you can do a lot of cleaning using natural things such as vinegar, water and lemon juice?
★ Remember to take a cloth bag or a 'bag for life' when you go shopping to avoid using a plastic bag.
★ Did you know that meat production uses much more energy than plants? Try eating vegetarian food for one day. There are lots of delicious recipes to try – some are in this book!
★ Take a refillable drinks bottle out with you instead of buying water or juice in plastic bottles.

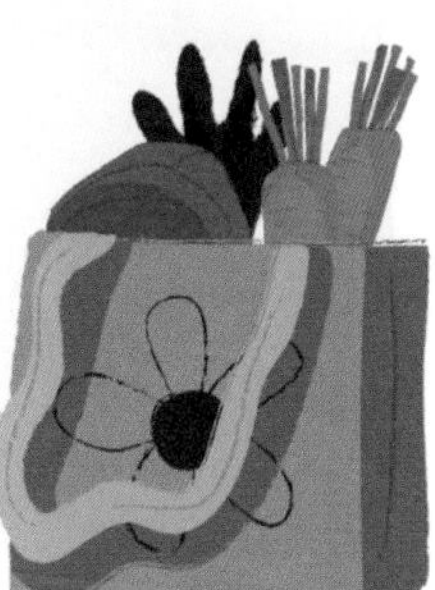

HOW DOES YOUR GARDEN GROW?

Once the weather warms up, April is a great time to start planting things. You don't need a big garden – in fact, you don't need a garden at all. A lot of flowers, fruits and vegetables can be planted in pots and grown on a windowsill or patio area.

Outdoors:

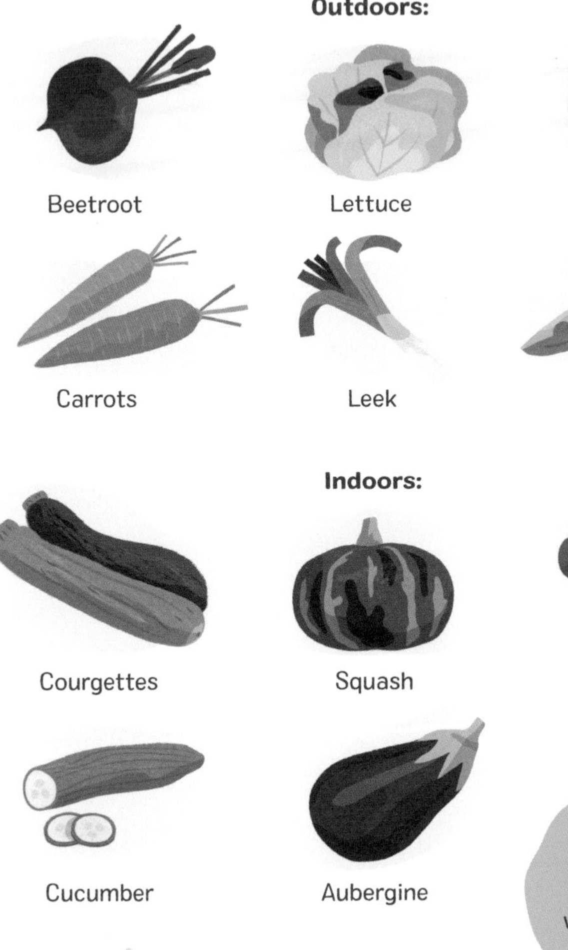

Beetroot

Lettuce

Strawberries

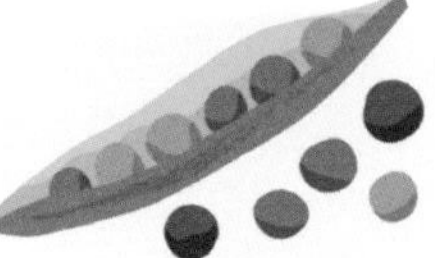

Carrots

Leek

Peas

Indoors:

Courgettes

Squash

Tomatoes

Cucumber

Aubergine

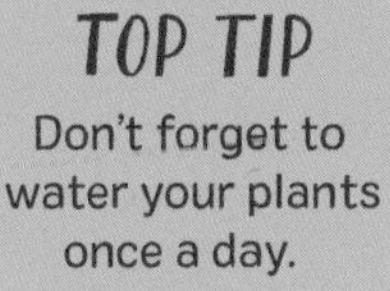

TOP TIP

Don't forget to water your plants once a day.

Recipe for *Broccoli Fritters*

A lot of people don't like eating broccoli, but these fritters are so tasty, everyone will be asking for seconds!

You will need:

Saucepan with lid
Sieve
Chopping board
Sharp knife
Mixing bowl
Metal spoon
Non-stick frying pan
Spatula

450 g broccoli florets
2 large eggs, beaten
65 g hard cheese, grated
4 tablespoons of plain flour
1 garlic clove, crushed
Salt and pepper
Vegetable oil

1. *Fill the saucepan with water and put the lid on. Then put it on the stove to boil.*
2. *Ask an adult to help you put the broccoli florets into the boiling water and cook them for 5 minutes.*
3. *Drain the broccoli in the sieve and put them on the chopping board.*
4. *Ask an adult to help you cut the broccoli into very small pieces.*
5. *In the mixing bowl, mix the chopped broccoli, beaten eggs, grated cheese, flour and garlic. Add salt and pepper.*
6. *Place the non-stick frying pan over a medium heat until hot.*
7. *Add the oil and make sure it covers the bottom of the pan in a thin layer.*
8. *Use the metal spoon to scoop out 2–3-tablespoon mounds of the broccoli mixture into the pan, then flatten the mounds slightly with the spatula and space them about 2 cm apart.*
9. *Cook the fritters for 2–3 minutes, flip them once, then cook them for an additional 1–2 minutes until they're golden brown and cooked through.*
10. *Serve warm with tomato ketchup, mayonnaise or sweet chilli sauce.*

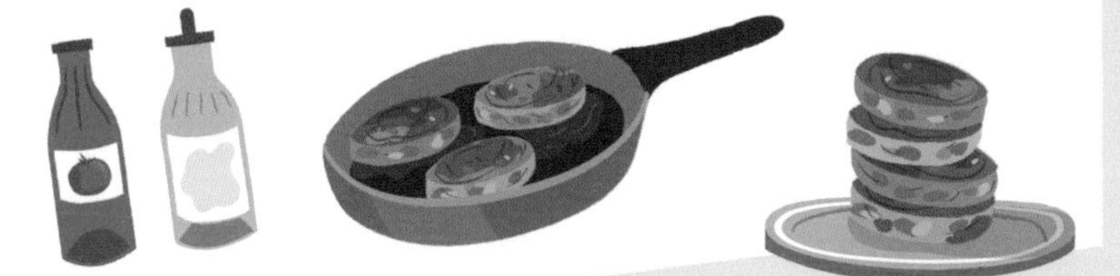

PARK LIFE

There's lots going on in local parks now that the days are longer and lighter. Why not join a park run? You don't have to be a fast runner, so you can chat as you run if you like! And there's often a park café nearby where you can go afterwards to have a well-earned snack and drink.

Look at the website **www.parkrun.org.uk** to find out where your nearest junior park run is. You will need to ask an adult to help you register online before you join a park run.

If running is not for you, take a scooter, skateboard or bike to the park. Or ask an adult if you can volunteer to walk a dog from your local dogs' home if there is one near you. (Or walk your own dog, of course!)

Whatever you choose to do, getting outside and breathing in the spring air will make you smile.

BIRDS ON THE MOVE

The birds are getting noisier now! You might find that you are woken up earlier by the sound of a wood pigeon cooing loudly outside your window. Then other smaller birds join in with their different sounds. This is called the 'dawn chorus'. If you've got time in the morning, it's lovely to lie in bed and just listen to the music the birds make – it's like having a free concert right outside your window!

More and more birds are finding their way back to Britain after the winter. Look out for the first swallows, swifts and house martins later in the month.

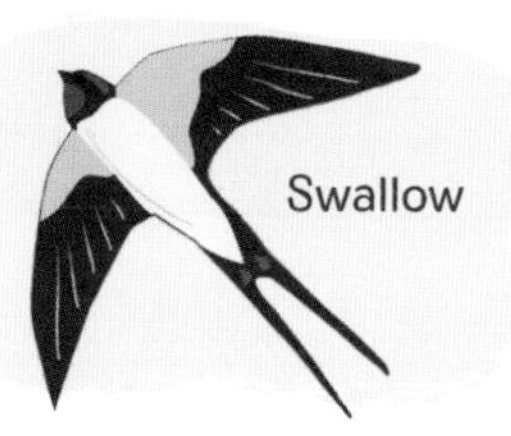

House martin

The bird that people think of most in April is the cuckoo. It spends the winter in Africa but comes back to Britain during this month.

Cuckoo

DID YOU KNOW...

★ It is traditional for people to write to *The Times* newspaper when they hear the first cuckoo of spring!
★ Each spring a female will lay between 12 and 22 eggs, all in other birds' nests.
★ A female cuckoo will lay her eggs in a nest belonging to the same kind of bird that looked after her when she was a chick.
★ Adult cuckoos move back to Africa as soon as their chicks are hatched. This can be as early as the end of June.
★ Young cuckoos follow their parents back to Africa several weeks later.

MAY

SPECIAL DAYS

1st Beltane (pagan celebration)/May Day

2nd Early May bank holiday

3rd Eid al-Fitr (end of Ramadan)

26th Ascension Day

ANNIVERSARIES

10 years ago . . .

On 18 May 2012, the Olympic flame arrived in Great Britain from Greece. This marked the opening of the 2012 Olympic Games in London.

115 years ago . . .

On 13 May 1907, the British writer Daphne du Maurier was born. She wrote many novels set in Cornwall, including *Rebecca*, *My Cousin Rachel* and *The Birds*.

"A swarm of bees in May
Is worth a load of hay."

Hedgerows are at their most beautiful in May. They are full of wildflowers which attract lots of insects and butterflies. The traditional saying above gives us a good picture of what is going on in nature in May. It is a very busy month for bees! They are working hard to gather nectar to feed on, and while they do this, they are also helping plants to grow through 'pollination'. So lots of busy bees in May means plenty of yummy fruit and vegetables for us. It's a good idea to plant wildflowers in your garden or allotment if you can, as this will feed the bees.

At the beginning of the month there is also an explosion of golden dandelions everywhere. Birds such as goldfinches love the seeds: you'll see lots of these beautiful birds flocking to nibble the seeds just before the flowers turn into dandelion 'clocks'.

Why is May Called May?

Nobody knows for sure, but it seems likely that this month was named after the Greek goddess Maia, who was goddess of fertility. Her festival is still celebrated by some people on 15th May.

Meteor Shower *Eta Aquariids*

These meteors usually fall sometime between 19th April and 28th May. This year, you should be able to see the shower from the night of 6th May to the morning of 7th May. About 30 meteors will fall each hour. The shower is formed by particles of dust left behind by Halley's Comet. This comet has been known about since ancient times and can be seen from Earth without using a telescope.

If you want to see the meteor shower, you will have to stay up late or get up very early! The best spot to see it from will be a very dark place from about midnight. The meteors can appear anywhere in the sky.

DID YOU KNOW...

4th May is Star Wars Day because "May the Fourth" sounds like "May the Force [be with you]". Many fans rewatch all the Star Wars films on this day!

FESTIVAL FUN

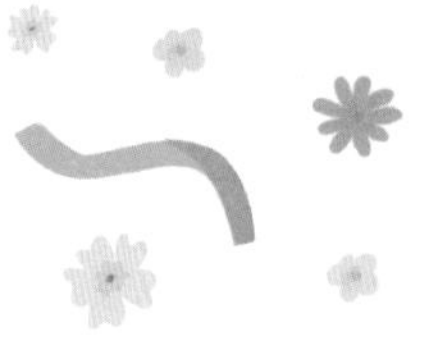

1st May *Beltane*

The old Gaelic word *Beltane* means 'bright fire'. This ancient pagan festival celebrates the return of summer and marks the time of year halfway between the spring equinox and the summer solstice.

Long ago, it was a time when farmers let their cows and sheep back out into the fields after the cold weather. Farmers lit big bonfires with special herbs inside. They would then make their animals walk in between the fires so that they could breathe in the purifying smells. This was supposed to protect them from illness.

1st May *May Day*

May Day celebrations are often mixed in with Beltane bonfires. A May queen is chosen and either two people carry her, or she rides through the streets on a cart pulled by a horse. The cart is covered in flowers and the May queen wears flowers in her hair. She sometimes has a man or boy with her representing the Green Man, who is the pagan god of nature. People dance around a maypole, which is a long stick with coloured ribbons coming from the top. Each person takes a ribbon and dances around the pole, weaving in and out of each other until the pole is tightly wrapped in the ribbons.

DID YOU KNOW...

'Hobby horses' are a May Day tradition. Originally a hobby horse was not just a model horse's head on a stick, like the toys you see today. It was a costume for the May Day parade which made the person wearing it look as though they were riding a real horse.

3rd May *Eid al-Fitr*

Eid al-Fitr is an Islamic festival that is celebrated by Muslims all over the world. It is the day which ends Ramadan and it falls on or near the date of a new moon. During Eid, Muslim people celebrate with delicious food, by praying and by giving money to charity.

26th May *Ascension Day*

Ascension Day is a Christian festival and a very important date in the Christian calendar. The word 'ascension' means 'rising up'. According to the *Bible*, 40 days after Easter Sunday Jesus ascended, or rose up, to heaven and went to sit at the right-hand side of God. Ascension Day is always celebrated on a Thursday. However, not all countries hold the feast on this day. In Germany, Father's Day is celebrated on the same day.

GATHERING BUDS IN MAY

May is the month for wild flowers. It seems as though nature finds any excuse to sprinkle the roadsides, paths, woodlands and parks with colour. Even the most boring journeys are made more enjoyable by looking out of the window at the burst of colour.

Why not take your nature notebook with you and note down or draw what you see? If you have permission from the owner of the flowers, you can also pick one or two and press them when you get home – but be careful not to pick too many as bees and other insects need flowers for food.

How to *Press Flowers*

You don't need a special flower press. You can simply use paper and a very heavy book!

1. *Take some sheets of newspaper and the biggest, heaviest book that you can find.*
2. *Lay the flowers on the newspaper, opening them out as much as you can without breaking them.*
3. *Put another sheet of newspaper on top of the flowers.*
4. *Open the heavy book near the end.*
5. *Put the newspaper sheets into the book.*
6. *Close it and make sure the heaviest part of the book is on top of the flowers.*
7. *Leave for two or three weeks.*
8. *The flowers will have dried out and be pressed very flat. They will be very delicate so take extra care when lifting them off the newspaper.*

TOP TIP

Use your dried flowers to make bookmarks or even add them to homemade paper.

Make *Homemade Paper*

This takes a couple of days to make as you need to soak the recycled paper in water overnight. You can add some of your pressed flowers as decorations.

You will need:

Used paper
Washing-up bowl
Water
Old pair of tights
Old wooden picture frame or wire coat hanger bent into a square
Food processor
Shallow baking tray
Decorations such as flowers, leaves and seed heads
Food colouring or paint
2 small old towels
Rolling pin
Pegs

1. *Collect any old paper you can find.*
2. *Place it in a washing-up bowl full of cold water and leave it overnight.*
3. *While the paper is soaking, cut the tights so that you have one layer of fabric and then stretch this over the picture frame or coat hanger to make a screen.*
4. *The next day, ask an adult to help you fill the food processor half full with water.*
5. *Add a handful of wet paper and whizz it up until it looks like a thick milkshake.*
6. *Pour the mixture into a baking tray and add the flowers, leaves and seed heads. Add food colouring or paint if you want.*
7. *Place your screen face-down in the mixture and gently move it around to coat it with an even amount of pulp.*
8. *Lift the screen out and let it drain on a draining board or over the washing-up bowl.*
9. *Once a lot of the water has dripped out, put the paper on an old towel, place another towel on top and use the rolling pin to squeeze out any water that is left.*
10. *Hang the paper up using pegs on the washing line or somewhere warm and dry.*

TOP TIP

Ask a grown-up to help you with the food processor.

BUTTERFLIES AND CATERPILLARS

We're Going on a Caterpillar Hunt!

Caterpillars are among the most fascinating of small creatures. They eat so much and grow so fast! And then, before you know it, they have turned into beautiful butterflies.

You will need:

Jar or small pot
Cling film with holes in
Magnifying glass or minibeast pot

How to find caterpillars:

1 *Look for holes in leaves and missing parts of plants. Caterpillars spend every moment of every day munching their way through leaf after leaf. Sometimes the holes are as big as your fingernail, sometimes they are tiny pinpricks – it depends on the size of the caterpillar.*

2 *Can you find any little black blobs on the leaves? These might be caterpillar poo. The proper name for them is 'frass'. If you see any, you'll know a caterpillar is nearby.*

3 *What about any tiny glassy green balls? These are butterfly or moth eggs, which means small caterpillars will soon be hatching.*

4 *Sometimes you might see strands of silk on a plant. It's not only spiders who spin silk, so do some caterpillars. They use them to make trails to walk around on or to make cocoons.*

When you find caterpillars, you can gently tip them into your pot to observe them. Don't forget to put some of the leaves you found them on into the pot so that your hungry caterpillars don't get even hungrier! Remember to return the caterpillars to where you found them, so that they can turn into beautiful butterflies or moths.

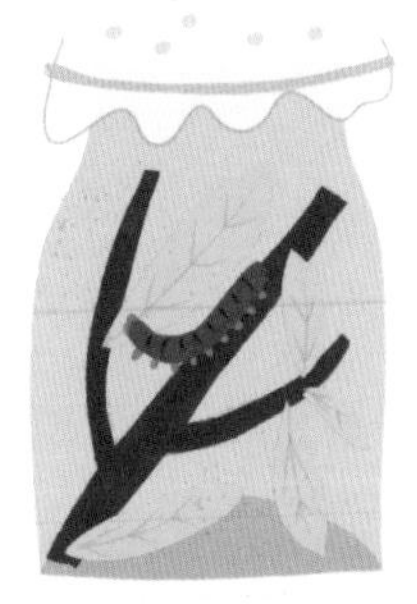

CAN YOU SPOT...

Common blue
Comma
Green-veined white
Brimstone
Speckled wood
Holly blue
Orange-tip
Clouded yellow
Brown argus
Red admiral
Painted lady
Large white (also called cabbage white)

COUNTRYSIDE CODE

Did you know that there are rules you should follow when you are out walking in the countryside? They are designed to make the countryside safe for everyone so that we can all enjoy it.

1 Respect the local community

Farmers work hard all year round to grow the food we eat and to look after their animals. If you see a farm animal, remember it is not a pet. Do not feed or stroke it. And if you are in a car or on a bike, make sure you slow down for farm animals so you don't frighten them.

2 Leave gates as you find them

If you walk up to a gate and it is closed, make sure you close it behind you. The farmer probably wants to keep the animals from running away. However, if you find a gate open, do not close it behind you as a farmer might be moving animals from one field to the next.

3 Stick to paths and follow signs

Some land is open to everyone to walk on, but some is private. If you are not sure, check a detailed map and follow the signs. This is for your own safety as well as to respect people's privacy and to help look after important habitats. You wouldn't want to walk into a field with an old mine shaft, or a pair of ground-nesting lapwings.

4 Leave no trace

Always take your litter away with you. Many places in the countryside do not have public bins but this doesn't mean you can drop your rubbish on the ground. Litter could start a wildfire and is dangerous to wildlife and farm animals as they can hurt themselves on it or end up eating it which could make them seriously ill.

5 Look after your dog

It is important to keep dogs under control in case they run into a field of farm animals and scare them. Look out for signs asking you to keep your dog on the lead. If you have to walk through a field of cows, your dog should be on a lead, but if you are approached by the cows, it would be better to let your dog off their lead. The dog will be safer and so will you. Always remember to pick up any mess your dog makes, too, and carry it to the nearest dog bin, as this can make farm animals sick!

TAKE ME TO THE RIVER

One of the most relaxing things you can do on a sunny day in May is to get out in a boat! There are many places all over Britain where you can hire kayaks, canoes, rowing boats or paddle boards. It is the best way to see river wildlife as you are usually moving slowly and quietly and you are at the same level as many of the animals, birds and insects. If you spot something up ahead, stop paddling and float slowly and quietly towards what you want to observe. It's a good idea to bring binoculars with you.

This is a perfect time of year for spotting brown trout which rise to the surface to eat the hatching mayflies. There will also be lots of little ducklings, cygnets, goslings and chicks around. Moorhen chicks have extremely fluffy black bodies with incredibly long legs and huge feet! You should also look out for kingfishers which will be hunting a lot at this time of year, catching fish, of course, but also tadpoles and damselflies.

Make a *River Memory Catcher*

This is a fun way to make a walk more interesting, and it's a great activity to do in any weather. Remember to take the string with you before you head out. When you get home, you can hang your memory catcher in your room!

You will need:

3 sticks of equal length
2.5 m wool, string or garden twine

1 *Find three sticks of equal length – they'll need to be about 30 cm long.*

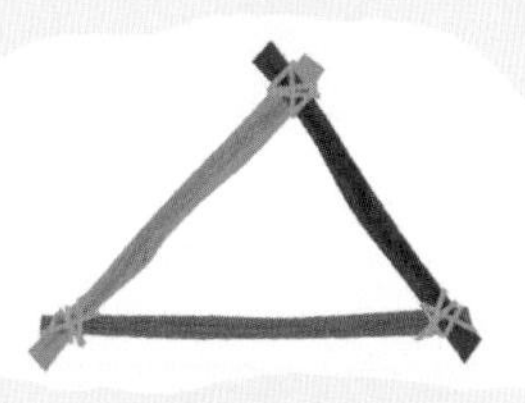

2 *Tie the sticks together using the wool, string or garden twine to make a triangle.*

3 *Wind the wool, string or garden twine around the triangle until you have created a sort of net or spider's web effect.*

4 *As you walk along the river, see what you can spot – birds, trees, flowers and so on. Then look out for things that you can easily pick up that will remind you of what you have seen – feathers, leaves, petals, even small stones.*

5 *Slot these into the web of string in your memory catcher – you can tie them in place if you have enough string left over. Try and find as many river walk memories as you can!*

JUNE

SPECIAL DAYS

2nd	Spring bank holiday
3rd	Platinum Jubilee Bank holiday
4th	Shavuot (Jewish festival of weeks)
5th	World Environment Day/Whitsun/ Pentecost (Christian celebration)
11th	The Queen's official birthday/ Trooping the Colour (the Queen's birthday parade)
19th	Father's Day
21st	Summer solstice
22nd	Windrush Day
24th	Midsummer's Day

ANNIVERSARIES

70 years ago . . .

On 26 June 1952, Olive Morris was born. She campaigned for the rights of Black people in South London and Manchester and helped to set up the Organisation of Women of African and Asian Descent and the Brixton Black Women's Group.

100 years ago . . .

On 10 June 1922, the actor Judy Garland was born. She is famous for playing the role of Dorothy in the film *The Wizard of Oz*.

> "At midnight, in the month of June,
> I stand beneath the mystic moon."
>
> EDGAR ALLAN POE (1809–1849)

Summertime is here at last! It's time for strawberries and cream and barbecues. The roses are out in the gardens and parks and, of course, there are lots of long, hot, sunny days to look forward to – right? Well . . . there will be some sunshine, but often we get excited and plan summer outdoor activities in Britain, only to find that the rain means we have to change our plans.

Nevertheless, this is the month to enjoy long days outside. When you get home from school it feels as though you have so much extra time to have fun! You can meet your friends in the park for football or just laze around chatting in the shade eating ice cream. June has the longest day of the year, so by 21st June you won't see the sun go down until around 10 p.m. The full moon occurs on 14th June, so you'll have to stay up late if you want to see it!

DID YOU KNOW . . .

According to traditional folklore, if you pick a rose at midsummer, it will keep fresh until Christmas!

Why is June Called June?

The month of June was probably named after the Roman god Juno. She was the wife of Jupiter, who was the king of the gods. Juno was the goddess of marriage. Some people think it is good luck to get married in June. The Anglo-Saxons called it *Sera Monath*, which means 'dry month'. (Maybe it didn't rain so much back then!)

June Birth Signs

Gemini The sign of the twins. Anyone born between 21st May and 21st June is a Gemini. They are supposed to be very chatty!

Cancer If your birthday is between 22nd June and 22nd July it is said that you are born under the sign of the crab, known as Cancer. Cancerians are believed to be shy, sensitive, loving and thoughtful.

Constellation of the Month

Cassiopeia was a vain queen in Greek mythology. The legend tells us that she was thrown into the sky as a constellation after enraging Poseidon, the god of the sea. She boasted to him that her daughter, Andromeda, was more beautiful than his sea nymphs. She should have known that it is never a good idea to make an ancient god angry!

FESTIVAL FUN

4th June *Shavuot*

Shavuot is a Jewish festival during which Jewish people remember the day that God gave the Prophet Moses the holy scriptures, the *Torah*. Jewish people believe that Moses received the *Torah* from God on a mountain called Mount Sinai in Israel.

Shavuot always comes 50 days after the second day of Pesach. Women and girls light candles to welcome in the holiday, and some Jewish people stay up all night learning the *Torah*.

All Jewish people go to the synagogue on the first day of Shavuot to hear the reading of the Ten Commandments. This is a list of laws for living a good life. They can be found in the Torah, the *Qu'ran* and in the *Bible*, too.

Challah is a special bread that Jewish people eat on Shabbat (the Sabbath) and at big Jewish festivals such as Shavuot. It is a beautiful, plaited, slightly sweet bread and is absolutely delicious! At Shavuot the challah represents the new year's wheat which people give thanks for.

Recipe for *Challah*

In honour of Shavuot, why not bake your own challah loaf? This recipe makes two loaves.

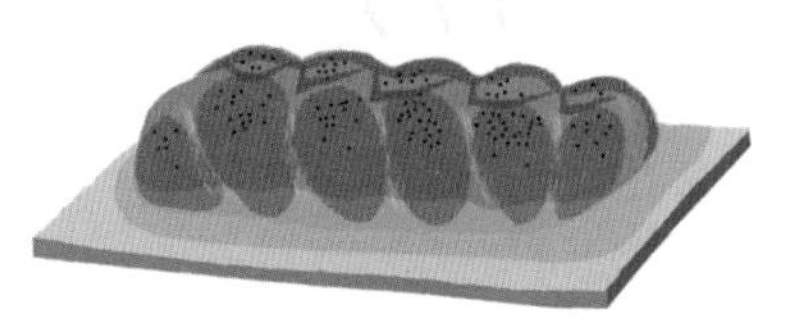

You will need:

Mixing bowl
Dough hook
Food mixer
Tea towel, damp
Baking tray
Pastry brush
Wire rack

4 tablespoons of caster sugar
1 tablespoon of salt
4 tablespoons of vegetable oil
300 ml warm water
1 tablespoon of dried active baking yeast
3 eggs, slightly beaten
750 g plain flour
1 egg, beaten (for glazing)
1 tablespoon of poppy seeds

1 *Place the sugar, salt and oil in the mixing bowl and fix the dough hook into the mixer.*

2 *Add the warm water, and stir into the sugar and salt until they have dissolved. Stir in the dried active yeast and then set aside for a few minutes.*

3 *Mix in the slightly beaten eggs.*

4 *Add about 500 g of the flour to the yeast mixture. Mix until the dough looks stringy.*

5 *Keep adding the rest of the flour until the dough has formed a ball on the dough hook. Let the hook continue to knead the dough for several minutes until the dough is smooth and elastic.*

6 *Turn the soft dough on to a lightly floured work surface and add the remaining flour. Knead the dough with your hands for about 8–10 minutes.*

7 *Use more vegetable oil to grease the mixing bowl, then place the dough into the bowl. Make sure the surface of the dough is completely coated with the oil. Cover the bowl with the damp tea towel and leave the dough to rise for about an hour.*

8 *Once it has risen, punch the air out of the dough and then leave it to rise again for about 45 minutes.*

9 *Preheat the oven to 180°C/160°C fan/Gas Mark 4.*

10 *Divide the dough in half, then divide each half into three equal parts and make two plaits.*

11 *Place both loaves on a greased baking tray. Cover with the tea towel and allow to rise until the loaves have doubled in size. Brush with the beaten egg and sprinkle with poppy seeds.*

12 *Bake for 35 minutes until golden brown.*

5th June *World Environment Day*

World Environment Day was set up in 1974 to encourage all of us, including governments and businesses, to look after our planet. Countries take it in turns to host and choose a theme for World Environment Day. For example, when Colombia was the host country, the theme was 'Time for Nature'. The focus was on 'biodiversity' which means the number and variety of all the living things on Earth. Colombia has a very high biodiversity, but because the Amazon rainforest is becoming smaller, the country wanted to raise awareness of the need to protect all life by stopping humans from chopping down the trees in the forest and damaging the natural habitat of everything that lives there.

TOP TIP

Plant wildflowers such as bluebells and foxgloves in your garden to encourage the bees to come!

5th June *Pentecost or Whitsun*

Pentecost or Whitsun is the seventh Sunday after Easter. On this day, Christians remember that God sent the Holy Spirit to be with the followers of Jesus. In the north-west of England some churches and chapels still hold 'Whit walks' – parades that include brass bands, choirs and girls dressed in white.

19th June *Father's Day*

Father's Day is a day to remember dads, and also grandfathers or other male relatives or carers who are special people in our lives. You could plan a camping trip with your relative or carer for a night. You don't have to go anywhere special – you could just camp in the garden. Or if it's raining, choose your favourite film to watch together.

21ST JUNE SUMMER SOLSTICE

"In winter I get up at night
and dress by yellow candle-light.
In summer, quite the other way,
I have to go to bed by day."

ROBERT LOUIS STEVENSON (1850–1894)

It can be very annoying when you have to go to bed when the sun is still up! It is particularly hard to go to sleep on the longest day of the year. Pagans traditionally do not go to bed at all on this night! They stay up to welcome the sunrise and give thanks for its power and warmth.

One famous pagan summer solstice celebration happens at Stonehenge, a circle of standing stones in Salisbury in the west of England. People meet at the stones to watch the sunrise at about 4.45 a.m. This is an act of worship and there is a lot of music and dancing.

The summer solstice is also known as *Litha*, which is an Anglo-Saxon word for 'midsummer'. Bonfires were lit on the tops of hills – some places in Britain still do this. The bonfire represents the strength, light and heat of the sun. Young men used to leap over them for luck!

WINDRUSH DAY

Windrush Day is on 22nd June. On this day in 1948, 1,027 people finally arrived in Britain after making the long journey, thousands of miles across the Atlantic, from the Caribbean on a ship called the *Empire Windrush*. They came because the British government had advertised jobs for them in Britain.

Lots of young men and women from the Caribbean had served in the British army, navy and air force during the Second World War. When the war ended, they were keen to come to Britain to help rebuild the cities after bombs had destroyed so much of the country. This was the first time so many people had come to Britain from the Caribbean, and many more came in the years that followed, to live with their families and to work here.

DON'T BE A GOOSEBERRY!

Gooseberries are funny little hard, hairy green fruit that don't look very attractive, and they grow on very spiky bushes, so you have to be careful and wear gardening gloves if you want to pick any yourself. They are ripe late in June and go on being edible into early July, depending where you are in the country. You can, of course, also find them in the shops around this time – without the spikes!

There are a few myths and sayings surrounding the poor old gooseberry. "Don't be a gooseberry," means, "Don't be left out – join in the fun!" This may be because of the green and spiky appearance of the fruit, which makes us think of someone who isn't friendly. Gooseberries used also to be known as fayberries because of the ancient belief that fairies used to hide in gooseberry bushes if they were frightened.

They may not look very nice raw, but gooseberries are delicious when stewed with sugar or used in cakes, jams and tarts. They are also a good source of vitamin C.

Recipe for

Gooseberry and Elderflower Jam

Green jam might not be your first choice of spread, but this is delicious!

You will need:

Small plate
Large saucepan
Wooden spoon
Oven gloves
Metal teaspoon
Ladle
Washed and sterilised jam jars
Greaseproof paper, cut into circles
Coloured cloth
Elastic band or ribbon or string

1 kg gooseberries
300 ml water
900 g granulated white sugar
100 ml elderflower cordial

1 *Put the small plate in the freezer before you start making the jam.*

2 *Tip the gooseberries into the large saucepan with 300 ml water.*

3 *Cook over a low heat for about 15 minutes, stirring occasionally until the fruit has broken down into a mushy purée.*

4 *Add the sugar and cook over a low heat until the sugar has dissolved.*

5 *Ask an adult to help you turn up the heat as high as it will go and boil everything for 10 minutes. Stir the bottom of the pan to make sure the jam doesn't burn.*

6 *Ask an adult to help you to skim off any scum that appears on the surface.*

7 *Take the plate from the freezer and put a teaspoonful of jam on it. After a couple of minutes, push your finger through the jam. If it wrinkles, your jam has set. If not, put the plate back in the freezer. Keep boiling the jam for two more minutes, then test again.*

8 *Once your jam has set, stir in the elderflower cordial.*

9 *Ladle the jam into the sterilised jars and place a circle of greaseproof paper on top of each jar, then cover with the lid. You can decorate the lid with a circle of coloured cloth and hold it in place with an elastic band or ribbon or string.*

HUG A TREE!

When you are out walking this month, take time to look at the trees you find. They will be in full leaf now, and will provide you with lots of cooling shade if you are walking on a hot day. Trees are very important for our environment. They are the biggest plants on the planet, and produce lots of oxygen for us to breathe. They also store carbon, make the soil rich and give life and a home to the world's wildlife. So give a tree a hug today and say thank you! They do a lot for us.

Ash

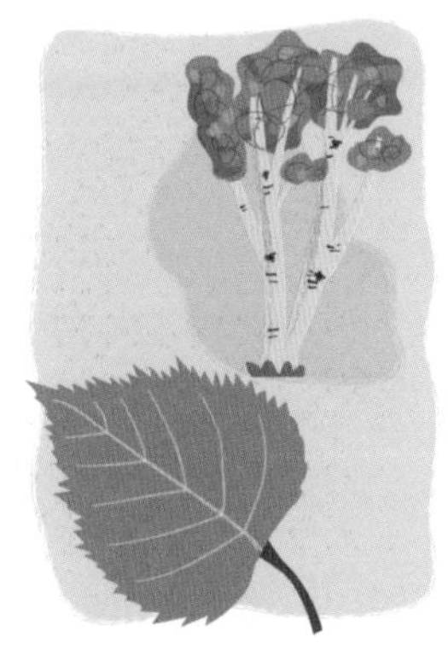

Silver birch

Oak

Beech

Sycamore

Horse chestnut

BARKING MAD FUN

This is the sort of activity you can do on a drizzly day as the branches and leaves will shelter you from a light shower. You can do it on a hot day, too, of course, as the branches and leaves will provide you with shade! Take a few sheets of paper and some crayons out into the woods or garden or out into your local park and have fun creating some beautiful colourful patterns. You could then use the paper as wrapping paper, make greetings cards from it or frame your lovely pattern with some twigs and give it as a gift.

Avoid this activity on windy days.

You will need:

Tree – or 2 or 3!
Plain paper
Wax crayons

1 *Choose an interesting tree. The big old knobbly ones are the best because the patterns in their bark are bigger.*
2 *Press the paper against the bark and hold it in place. You might need to ask a grown-up to help you keep it steady.*
3 *Press your crayon sideways firmly against the paper and rub until the pattern starts to come through. Try not to press too hard, or you'll rip the paper.*
4 *When the pattern has come through, remove the paper.*

JULY

SPECIAL DAYS

9th	Eid al-Adha (Muslim celebration)
10th	Sea Sunday (Christian celebration)
12th	Battle of the Boyne (Northern Ireland)
15th	St Swithun's Day
25th	St James's Day (Grotto Day)
30th	Muharram (Islamic New Year)

ANNIVERSARIES

15 years ago . . .

On 2 July 2007, Baroness Warsi was made a peer. She had been the first female Muslim to attend government Cabinet Meetings. At her first meeting in Downing Street she wore a traditional South Asian salwar kameez (a loose-fitting tunic and wide-legged trousers).

50 years ago . . .

On 1 July 1972, the first Gay Pride Rally took place in London. People gathered to raise awareness of the need for everyone to be treated the same. The movement is now called Pride to include all LGBT+ people.

"In scorched July
The storm-clouds fly."

CHRISTINA ROSSETTI (1830–1894)

At last the school holidays are here – weeks and weeks of free time to do whatever you like! It would be wonderful if we could rely on the weather to be fine for the whole of the holidays, but July can be a particularly stormy month. In fact, you are more likely to experience a thunderstorm during this month than at any other time during the year. This is because storms develop when there is a layer of warm air near the ground underneath a layer of much colder air. This is much more common in the summer when the days are longer, as there is more sunshine and therefore more energy.

But don't worry – there will still be golden days when you can rush to the beach or have long, lazy picnics in the park. And when the weather does break, just pull on some waterproof clothes and go out to splash in the puddles and breathe in the lovely smell of summer rain!

Why is July Called July?

It was named to honour the Roman statesman Julius Caesar as it was the month in which he was born (12th July). Before that, it was known as *Quintilis* – Latin for 'fifth' – as this was the fifth month in the Roman year before the calendar was changed. The Anglo-Saxons called it *Heymonath* as this is haymaking time.

Phases of the Moon in July 2022

First Quarter	Full Moon	Last Quarter	New Moon
7th July	13th July	20th July	28th July

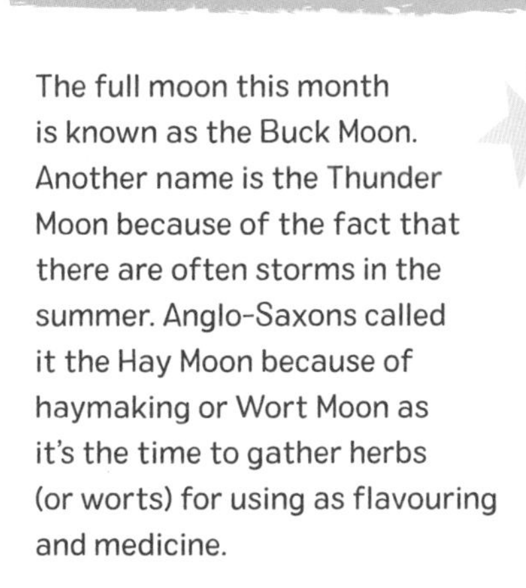

The full moon this month is known as the Buck Moon. Another name is the Thunder Moon because of the fact that there are often storms in the summer. Anglo-Saxons called it the Hay Moon because of haymaking or Wort Moon as it's the time to gather herbs (or worts) for using as flavouring and medicine.

DID YOU KNOW...

The Buck Moon gets its name from the new antlers that grow every summer from a buck (male) deer's forehead.

FESTIVAL FUN

9th July *Eid al-Adha*

This is an Islamic festival that marks the end of the *hajj* pilgrimage to the holy city of Mecca. It commemorates how Ibrahim was willing to sacrifice his son Isma'il to God. Allah stopped the sacrifice and gave Ibrahim a lamb to kill instead. A version of this story is also found in the Jewish *Torah* and the Old Testament of the Christian *Bible*.

Many Muslims wear new clothes or their nicest outfits for this festival and attend a prayer service at a mosque. They also send Eid cards to family and friends, donate money to charity, and give each other gifts.

10th July *Sea Sunday*

Sea Sunday is usually held on the second Sunday in July. It is a Christian festival, mainly celebrated by people who live by the sea. On this day, people go to church to say prayers and give thanks for their friends and family members who go out in all weathers to work at sea. Charities and organisations such as the Sailors' Society and the Sea Cadets hold parades and fundraising events.

15th July *St Swithun's Day*

On St Swithun's Day there is a saying:

"St Swithun's Day, if thou dost rain,
for forty days it will remain.
St Swithun's Day, if thou be fair,
for forty days 'twill rain nae mair."

Thankfully, this is rarely true! St Swithun was the Bishop of Winchester. When he died in 862 CE, he was buried in front of the west door of the old Saxon cathedral building because he had said he wanted to be buried outdoors. He lay there for over 100 years. When another bishop came along in 971 CE, he wanted to have a new patron saint, so he dug up poor old St Swithun on his feast day, 15th July, and moved him to a tomb inside! That day there was a terrible storm which lasted for 40 days and 40 nights. Many people believed that this happened because the saint was not happy about being moved indoors, so that is where the saying about the weather comes from.

25th July *St James's Day or Grotto Day*

There is an old tradition that on St James's Day, children would make 'grottoes' or little caves out of seashells. This is because the scallop shell is supposed to be the symbol for St James, who was one of the followers of Jesus.

Whitstable Oyster Festival begins on St James's Day. An old Kentish tradition says that Julius Caesar went to Britain because he loved the Whitstable oysters! The festival is a celebration of thanksgiving that still survives today.

Make a *Seashell Grotto*

If you go to the seaside this month, you'll be sure to collect some shells from the beach. Why not make your own St James's grotto by the sea? Make a sandcastle and then decorate it with as many different kinds of shells and pebbles as you can find.

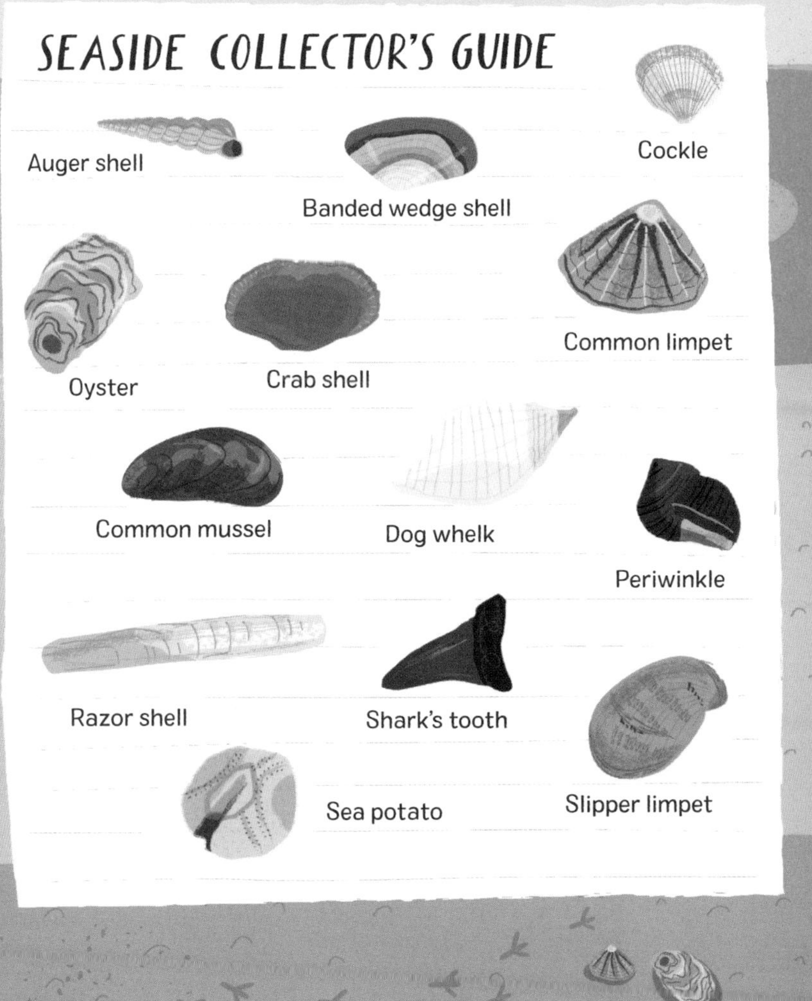

BUSY, BUZZY BEES!

There are more types of bee than you probably realised! Here are some of the ones you'll see in Britain:

Honeybee

Garden bumblebee

Patchwork leafcutter bee

Red mason bee

Red-tailed bumblebee

Common carder bee

Tree bumblebee

Honeybees are extremely important pollinators for flowers, fruits and vegetables. This means that they help plants grow! Bees transfer pollen between the male and female parts of a plant, and plants can then grow seeds and fruit.

Top Five Bee Facts

★ There are more than 25,000 different species of bee in the world!
★ Male honeybees in the hive are called drones and they do not have a stinger.
★ Worker honeybees are females. They do all the different tasks needed to operate and maintain the hive.
★ An average beehive can hold around 50,000 honeybees.
★ The queen bee lays all of the eggs in a colony. At the height of the season, she may lay over 2,500 eggs per day!

DOWN ON THE RIVER

Swan Upping

During the third week of July, the tradition of 'Swan Upping' takes place on the River Thames. This is a ceremony in which mute swans are caught by people in special boats called 'skiffs'. The swans are then 'ringed', which means they have numbered rings put on their legs so that we know how many swans there are. They are then released back to the river.

River Clean-Up

There are 'clean-ups' in rivers all over the UK. These are organised events in which people come together to help clear away plastic and other rubbish which sadly finds its way into rivers and streams and causes all kinds of problems for the wildlife that lives there.

Getting involved in a clean-up is a lot of fun if you get together with your friends and make a day of it. The events often happen in secret natural spaces which you might not have been to before. It also gives you a chance to help save the environment and make life better for wild animals. You can take the plastic you find to recycling centres or supermarkets which will take plastic bags and film wrap as well as bottles and cans.

If you want to find a clean-up near you, go to **www.ukrivers.net** and follow the links, or if you are near the Thames or any of the rivers and streams which flow into the Thames, look at **www.thames21.org.uk** for more information.

NAME THAT MINIBEAST!

If you can get to a canal, river, lake or pond, this is a great way to spend a summer afternoon, whatever the weather. In fact, minibeasts are sometimes easier to find on a rainy day, so if it's a typical wet and windy British summer day, just wrap up in your waterproofs, pull on a pair of wellies and get outside for some minibeast fun!

You will need:

Fishing net
Bucket
Magnifying glass (optional)
This book!

> **TOP TIP**
> You'll need an adult to help you with this activity if you are near deep water.

First of all, you need to fill your bucket with some water from the river, canal, lake or pond that you are visiting. Then put your net into the river and drag it back and forth gently. Once you have picked up a few minibeasts, tip them quickly and carefully into your bucket.

Now follow this guide to see what you might have found:

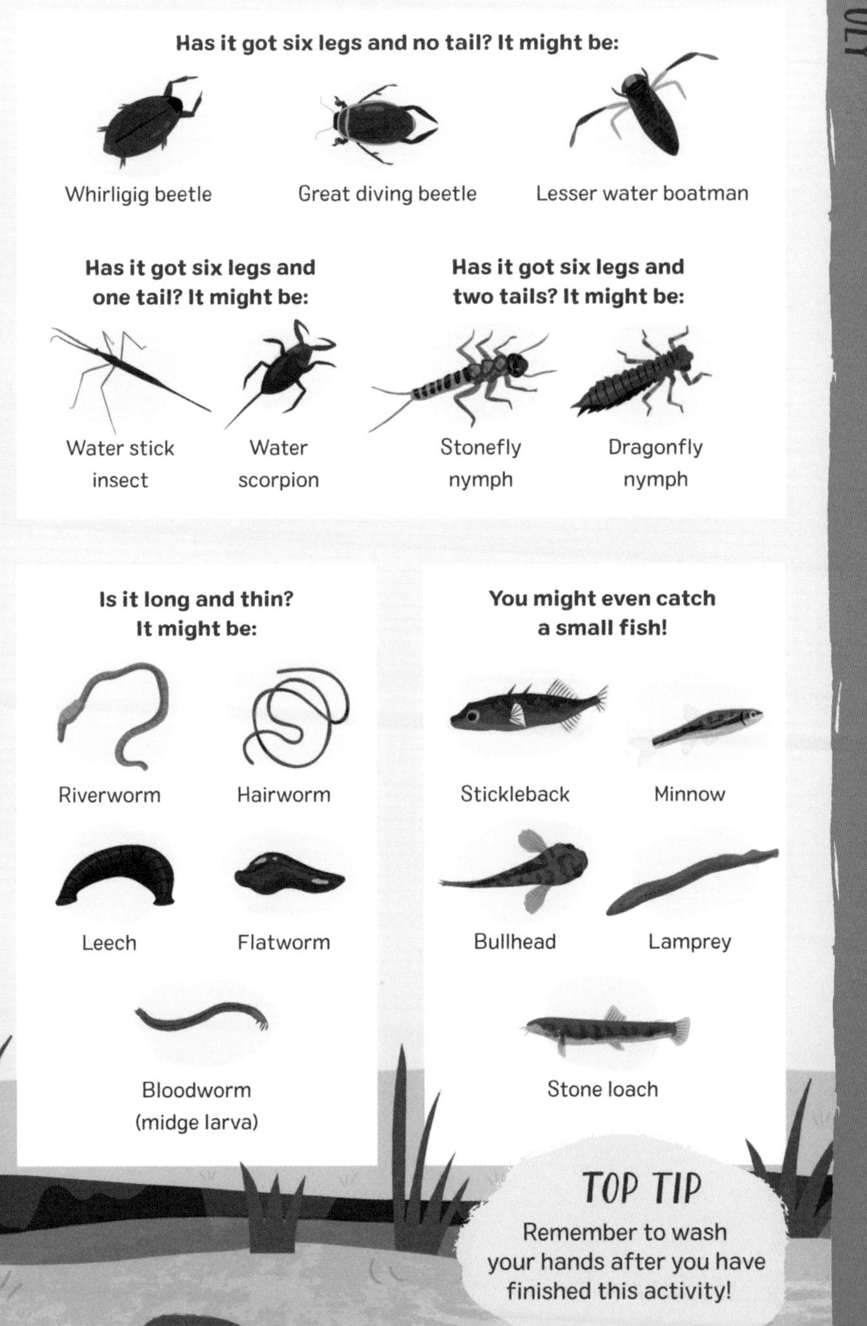
Has it got six legs and no tail? It might be:
Whirligig beetle
Great diving beetle
Lesser water boatman
Has it got six legs and one tail? It might be:
Water stick insect
Water scorpion
Has it got six legs and two tails? It might be:
Stonefly nymph
Dragonfly nymph
Is it long and thin? It might be:
Riverworm
Hairworm
Leech
Flatworm
Bloodworm (midge larva)
You might even catch a small fish!
Stickleback
Minnow
Bullhead
Lamprey
Stone loach
TOP TIP
Remember to wash your hands after you have finished this activity!

OUT IN THE GARDEN

There are lots of jobs to do now that the weather is warmer. The most important job you can help with is watering the plants if there hasn't been enough rain. It is always best to do the watering in the evening because if the day gets hot, the water can evaporate too quickly and the poor plants can get burnt. Tomato plants and runner beans need a lot of water at this time of year. So do any flowers you have growing in pots.

Another fun job you can help with is picking fruit – just don't eat too much as you pick! Lots of berries and currants will ripen this month: gooseberries, redcurrants, blackcurrants and raspberries. Plums, nectarines, peaches and apricots are also in season.

When you've finished all your gardening jobs, find a lovely cool spot in the shade to rest. If you have two trees that are close enough together, you could ask an adult to help you put up a hammock, or you could make a canopy instead by tying some string between two trees and hanging a sheet over it. Put a rug or some cushions under the sheet and you have a beautiful, cool canopy where you can read a book or have an afternoon snooze – or relax with a slice of yummy homemade cheesecake!

Recipe for *Easy Blackcurrant Cheesecake*

This easy, delicious dessert can be kept in the fridge one or two days before serving.

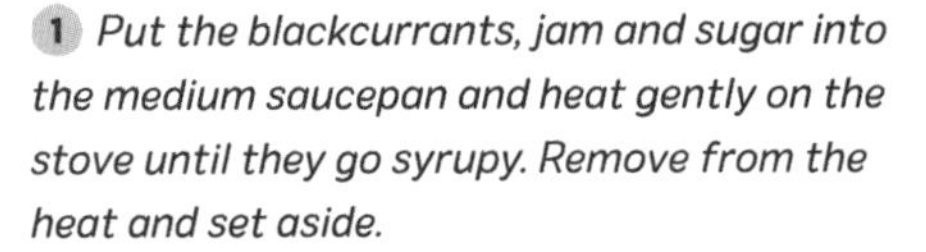

You will need:

Medium saucepan
Food processor
2 small saucepans
23 cm springform cake tin, greased
Metal spoon
Pyrex or heatproof bowl
Mixing bowl
Wooden spoon
Whisk

300 g blackcurrants
2 tablespoons of blackcurrant jam
5 tablespoons of caster sugar
250 g digestive biscuits
100 g butter
300 g white chocolate
250 g mascarpone
250 g cream cheese
300 ml double cream

1 *Put the blackcurrants, jam and sugar into the medium saucepan and heat gently on the stove until they go syrupy. Remove from the heat and set aside.*

2 *Whizz the biscuits in the food processor until you make fine crumbs.*

3 *Melt the butter on a low heat in a small saucepan.*

4 *Mix the biscuit crumbs into the melted butter and pour the mixture into the greased cake tin, patting it down with the metal spoon to make a smooth base layer.*

5 *Fill a small saucepan with water and bring it to simmering point on a medium heat.*

6 *Break the white chocolate into squares, put them in the Pyrex or heatproof bowl, then carefully put this over the simmering water until the chocolate has melted.*

7 *In the mixing bowl, beat together the mascarpone, cream cheese and double cream with the wooden spoon until smooth, then whisk in the melted white chocolate.*

8 *Take half of the blackcurrant mixture and fold it in gently with a wooden spoon until the white mixture is streaked with purple.*

9 *Pour this on to the biscuit base and put the cake into the fridge. Leave for 3–4 hours.*

10 *Take the cake out of the tin and put it on a plate. Pour over the remaining blackcurrant mixture to serve.*

TOP TIP

If you have a microwave, you can use that to melt the white chocolate instead of step 6.

AUGUST

SPECIAL DAYS

1st Lammas/Lughnasadh (pagan celebrations)/ Summer bank holiday (Scotland)

11th Raksha Bandhan (Hindu celebration)

28th Notting Hill Carnival

29th Summer bank holiday (England, Northern Ireland and Wales)

30th Ganesh Chaturthi (Hindu celebration)

ANNIVERSARIES

90 years ago . . .

On 22 August 1932, the BBC broadcasted the first television programme. It was just an experiment, so not very interesting to watch!

135 years ago . . .

On 3 August 1887, the poet Rupert Brooke was born. He is best known for his poems about the First World War such as 'The Soldier'.

225 years ago . . .

On 30 August 1797, the writer Mary Shelley was born. She is famous for her novel *Frankenstein*.

"In August when the days are hot,
I like to find a shady spot."

In August, it can feel as though the summer holidays will stretch on forever. You can enjoy the long, sunny days and spend as much time outside as possible. Perhaps you will be lucky enough to go to another country for your holiday, but if not there is more than enough to do closer to home. Days by the seaside or down by the river or playing in the parks or woods near your home offer lots of opportunities for activities and fun things to do with your friends and family.

Or perhaps you are the sort of person who likes to do nothing at all on a hot, sunny day? Sometimes it's lovely just to find a spot of shade where you can read or snooze or sit and watch the world go by. Whatever you choose to do this August, make the most of all your free time and enjoy yourself!

Why is August Called August?

The Roman Emperor Augustus Caesar thought that since there was a month named after his great-uncle Julius there should be one named after him, too! So *Sextilis* or the 'sixth month', was changed to August in the year 8 BCE in his honour.

The Anglo-Saxons called it *Weodmonath*, which means 'weed month' as so many weeds grow at this time of year.

Birth Flower and Birthstone

The flower for this month is the poppy, which represents strength, love, marriage and family. The stone is called peridot. It is an unusual olive-green colour and contains a lot of iron. Peridot is formed in the magma of volcanoes and comes to the surface when volcanoes erupt.

AUGUST BIRTH SIGNS

Leo Some people believe that anyone with a birthday which falls between 23rd July and 22nd August is born under this sign. They are said to be enthusiastic, passionate and generous.

Virgo It is said that people with a birthday between 23rd August and 22nd September are born under this sign. Virgos are thought to be good friends, kind and sensitive.

Constellation of the Month

You can see the constellation of Pegasus in the east in the early evening. It is a square of four very bright stars with trailing 'legs' and a 'head' coming off it. The brightest of the four main stars is called *Epsilon Pegasi* and is an orange supergiant. The star's name in Arabic is *Enif*, meaning 'nose', because it marks the place where Pegasus's nose is meant to be.

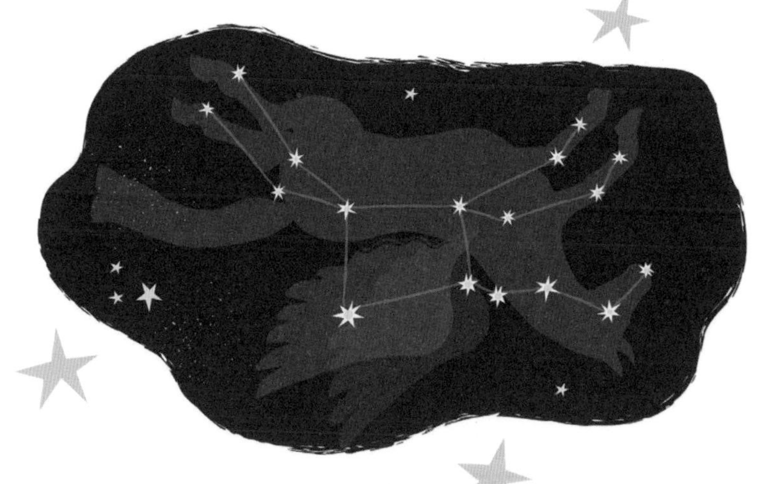

FESTIVAL FUN

1st August *Lammas*

Lammas is a pagan celebration of the first harvest, and is a time for giving thanks. The word *lammas* comes from the phrase 'loaf mass' which is a special celebration of the first grain to be cut in the harvest, and the first loaf to be made from that grain.

Lammas is also the name of the grain goddess, harvest queen and Earth mother. The harvest god is called John Barleycorn.

1st August *Lughnasadh*

On this day there is also an old Celtic festival called *Lughnasadh* – the festival of *Lugh* or *Lug*, the Celtic sun king and god of light. The celebrations include feasting, market fairs, games, bonfire celebrations and circle dancing. This is a time to remember that the power and energy of Lugh (the sun) is now slowing down and the darker days of winter are just around the corner.

11th August *Raksha Bandhan*

This is a Hindu festival celebrated at the full moon. The name *Raksha Bandhan* means the 'bond of protection'. *Raksha* means 'protection'and *Bandhan* means 'to tie'. The festival celebrates the relationship between brothers and sisters. During the festival, sisters tie a *rakhi* (holy thread) around their brothers' wrists as a symbol to show that they are praying for their brothers' protection and care. The brothers in return vow to look after their sisters, and give them a present.

30th August *Ganesh Chaturthi*

Today is the day that Hindus start celebrating the birthday of Lord Ganesh, the god with the head of an elephant. Communities get together to worship, have parties and decorate their houses with models and pictures of Lord Ganesh. He is known as the god of new beginnings and is supposed to bring prosperity, good fortune and success.

At the beginning of the celebrations, models of Ganesh are put up on high platforms in the home, or they are placed in beautifully decorated outdoor tents. These models are covered with yellow and red flowers and red paste made from sandalwood. They are also given presents of special homemade sweets.

FIRE, FIRE, BURNING BRIGHT

The Celtic festival of Lughnasadh is in August. It is a festival of light which includes bonfires and feasting. Why not make the most of the last days of summer by having a barbecue on your patio or in the garden? August might be the last chance for you to do this before the autumn sets in! Remember to ask an adult to help.

If you don't have a garden or patio big enough to do this, you can still enjoy the feasting part of Lughnasadh! Have a go at making these delicious veggie burgers indoors instead, then wrap them in foil and take them to the park or beach and enjoy them on one of those lovely long summer evenings. Remember to take any litter home with you so that you 'leave no trace' – the wildlife and plants will thank you for it!

Recipe for *Tasty Halloumi Burgers*

You will need:

Barbecue and charcoal (optional)
Pastry brush
Tongs

250 g halloumi cheese, cut into 8 slices
Tablespoon of olive oil
4 burger buns, split open
4 tablespoons of hummus
1 or 2 large tomatoes, sliced
Crunchy lettuce such as iceberg or little gem
Ketchup or any other sauces you like!

TOP TIP

Large Portobello mushrooms also go well with the halloumi and are a great replacement for a meaty burger.

1 *If using a barbecue, ask an adult to help you lay the charcoal and light it. You'll need to leave the charcoal to go white before you start cooking.*

2 *Brush both sides of all the slices of halloumi with the olive oil.*

3 *Barbecue or grill the cheese on both sides until it is just golden brown. Do not overcook.*

4 *This should take only 2 or 3 minutes each side. Use the tongs to turn the cheese.*

5 *Toast the burger buns if you like, but again, only for 2 or 3 minutes.*

6 *Spread hummus on one half and any other sauce you fancy on the other half: ketchup, mayonnaise, chilli sauce, brown sauce – your choice!*

7 *Add a couple of slices of halloumi, the tomato and the lettuce. You can add other toppings, too. Avocado also goes well with this.*

8 *Pop the other half of the bun on top and sink your teeth into this delicious summer treat!*

SPRING AND NEAP TIDES

A 'spring tide' does not only occur in the springtime! It is the name for the highest tide of the month, which in turn produces the lowest tide as its opposite. A 'neap tide' is the lowest high tide of the month and the highest low tide – this means that a neap tide shows the least difference between its high and low tides.

TOP TIP

It is a good idea to check the tides before you go swimming or take a boat out on the sea. You can do this online or you can buy tide times booklets from your local seaside town.

The moon affects the sea's tides. The tide changes every six hours, so if the tide is at its lowest (or the sea has 'gone out') at six in the morning, the tide will be at its highest again at midday.

ROCK POOLING

Who doesn't love the seaside on a hot summer's day? Even if you can't swim, perhaps you could find some rock pools to explore? The best time to do this is at low tide on a calm day when the sea has gone out and left water behind in the dips and hollows between the rocks. There's a lot to see in these miniature underwater worlds, so make sure you take your nature notebook with you – and try not to drop it in the water! Take a net and a bucket, too – that way you can take a closer look at some of the sea's minibeasts.

Remember to always be kind to the creatures you find and return them to their rock-pool homes after you have looked at them.

WATCH OUT, THERE'S A JELLY ABOUT!

No one likes to come across a jellyfish while they are swimming, so it is probably not going to be good news to you that we are seeing more and more of them on our beaches! This is because of climate change, which is making our oceans warmer than they used to be, so jellyfish are able to move into areas that were once too cold for them. Also, the oxygen levels in the sea have fallen by about 2 per cent over the last 50 years, and this means that jellyfish now have the perfect environment in which to live. On top of all this, we have been taking too many fish out of the seas, so that fish such as tuna, which would normally eat jellyfish, are not such a danger to them any longer.

The six types of jellyfish found in British waters are:

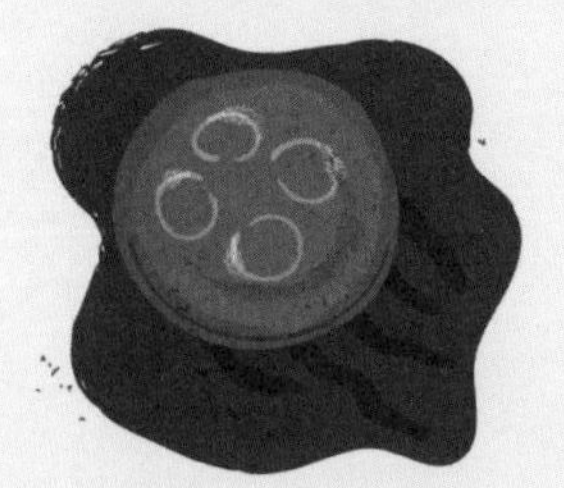

Moon jellyfish
(UK-wide)

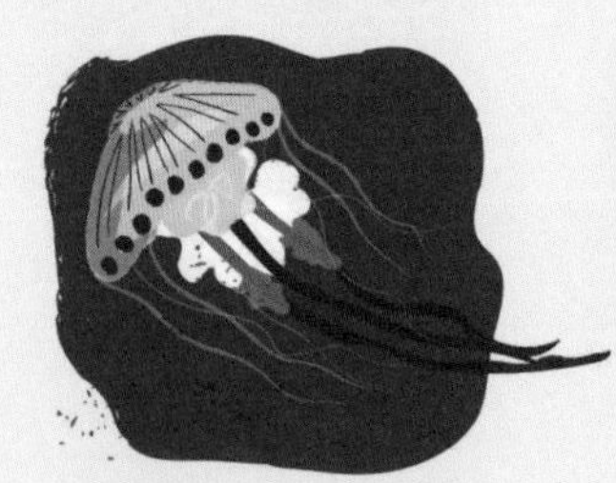

Compass jellyfish
(mainly in the South)

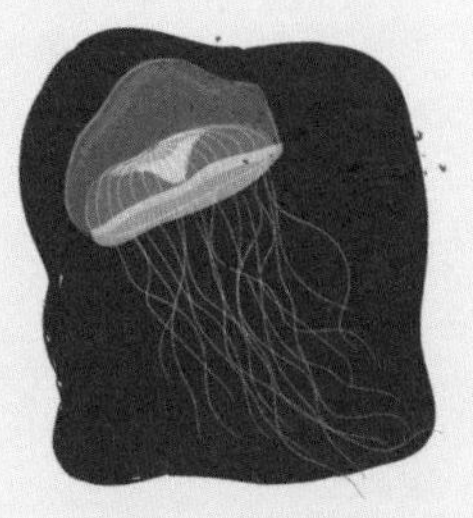

Blue jellyfish
(common in the South West and Wales)

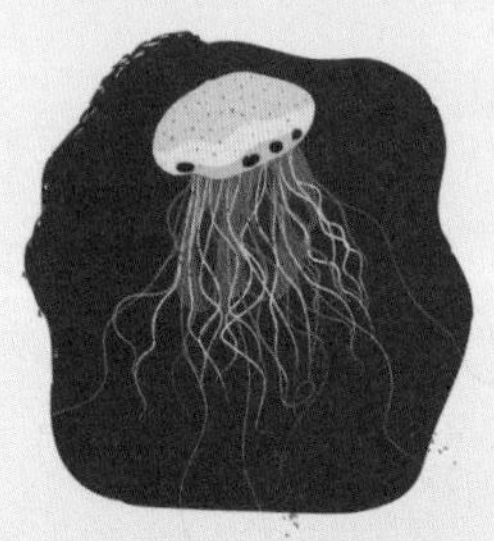

Lion's mane jellyfish
(North Wales, North of Scotland)

Barrel jellyfish
(the South West, Ireland, Wales, West of Scotland)

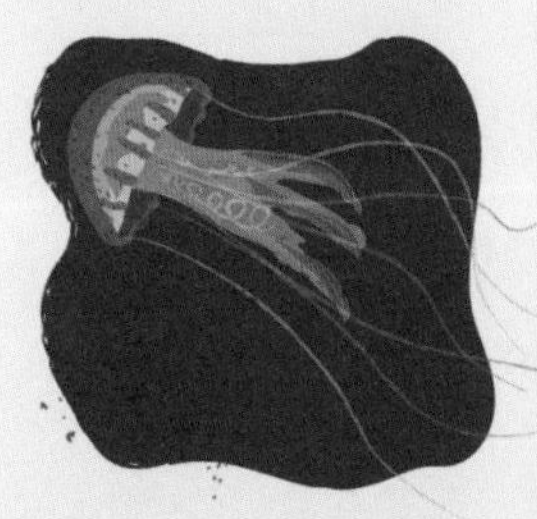

Mauve stinger jellyfish
(rare but can be found along the south coast)

DID YOU KNOW...

In Britain you are likely to see up to six different types of jellyfish and two species of jellyfish-like animals called the Portuguese man-of-war and the by-the-wind sailor. These last two are often confused with jellyfish but are actually 'siphonophores'.

UK jellyfish and siphonophores are not considered to be dangerous. However, some species can have a nasty sting. Their stings can range from mild, like the moon jellyfish, to very powerful, like the Portuguese man-of-war, which has the worst sting of all the jellyfish-like animals.

Portuguese man-of-war

By-the-wind sailor

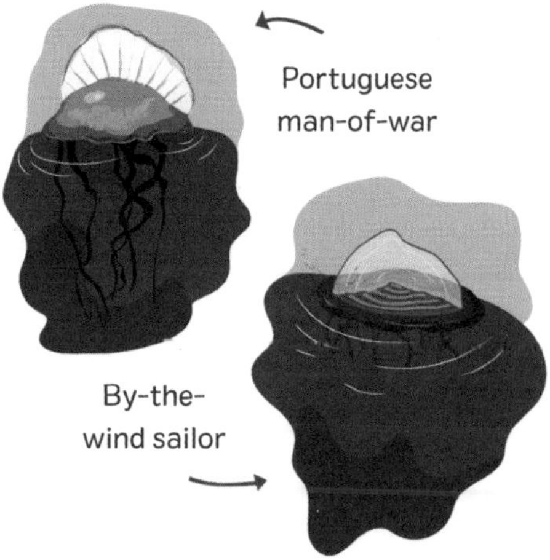

If you are stung by a jellyfish, here are some things you can do to relieve the pain:

★ Use seawater to rinse the area that was stung. Don't use fresh water, as this will make the sting worse.
★ If you can see the stinging spines from the jellyfish on your skin, ask an adult to pull them off carefully with tweezers.
★ Applying heat helps: you could soak the area in very warm water (as hot as you can stand) or you could press a hot flannel or towel gently over the sting.
★ Painkillers such as paracetamol or ibuprofen will help, but never take these without asking an adult first.
★ If the pain isn't going away and it is very bad, you should go to a minor injuries unit.

CAMPING

Sleeping outdoors is one of the most fun activities for friends and family to enjoy during the warm summer months. You don't have to go away and stay on a campsite. If you have a garden, why not camp there? You can have just as much fun. And if you get a bit chilly, you can creep indoors and get back into your own bed! But after you've tried all these things, you won't want to go back inside . . .

1 Go on a nature walk

Once you have pitched your tent, go for a walk as the sun is setting. Listen to all the sounds around you. Which birds can you hear? What can you see? Try to walk around as quietly as you can so that you don't frighten any of the wildlife. You might hear owls or see a badger or a fox.

2 Cook over the campfire

This is the best bit about camping! Don't forget to pack a box of matches with your camping things. Then, while you are on your nature walk, gather some small, dry sticks. You can use these to start your fire. Stick a sausage on a skewer or make campfire bread by mixing flour, water and a pinch of salt into a thick dough and wrapping it around a clean stick. Then carefully hold the food over the flames until it is cooked. Marshmallows make a perfect dessert.

③ Tell stories and sing songs by the fire

Once you have had enough to eat, enjoy the warmth of the fire and the way the flames flicker and make shadows. It's just the right atmosphere for having a good singalong. Or maybe, if you're feeling brave, you could get someone to tell ghost stories! Always make sure that you put out the fire completely when you are finished by pouring water over the embers. Never light a fire during periods of very dry weather as it could get out of control.

④ Play torchlight tag

If you're getting a bit chilly, a game of tag will warm you up. Make sure you all have torches so that you don't trip over anything. It's fun to chase each other's torchlight in the dark!

⑤ Look at the stars

Before you crawl into your snug sleeping bag, look up at the night sky. You will know quite a lot about the constellations by now, so see if you can spot any of the ones you have learnt about in this book.

SEPTEMBER

SPECIAL DAYS

23rd Autumn equinox/Mabon (pagan celebration)/Harvest festival (Christian celebration)

25th Rosh Hashanah (Jewish festival)

29th Michaelmas Day (Christian celebration)

ANNIVERSARIES

45 years ago . . .

Steve Biko died in South Africa on 12 September 1977. He worked hard to end the racist system of apartheid which kept black and white people from mixing.

200 years ago . . .

On 27 September 1822, a Frenchman called Jean-François Champollion proved to the world that he had decoded ancient Egyptian hieroglyphs using the Rosetta Stone. The stone said the same thing in three different languages, one of which was Ancient Greek. Using his understanding of the Greek, Champollion worked out what the Egyptian hieroglyphs represented.

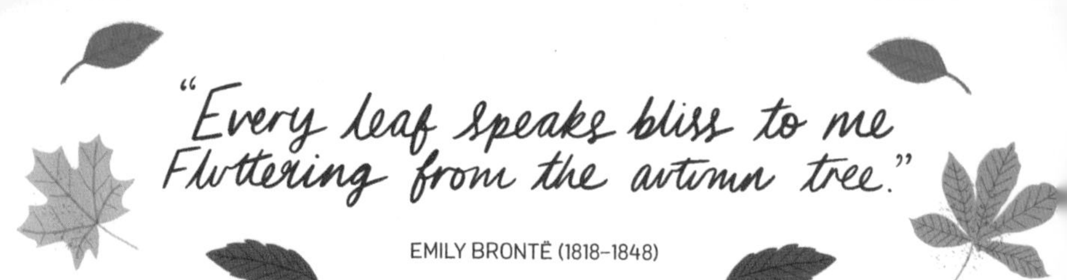

September can be a golden month. Summer is fading, yes, but there is still warmth in the air, and the leaves on the trees are slowly turning from their different shades of green to the fiery colours of autumn. And, of course, the end of summer means the beginning of school again, which not everyone is happy about! But the days are still long enough to allow some time for fun in the park after school, so make the most of it before the clocks change and the countdown to winter begins.

Why is September Called September?

This month kept its original name from the Roman calendar. September comes from the Latin word *septem*, which means 'seven'. September was the seventh month in the year when the calendar began with March instead of January.

Constellation of the Month

Cygnus means 'swan' in Latin. The Romans took the word from the Greek *kyknos*. The ancient Greeks had many stories about swans. One of them was about the tragic hero Orpheus. He was killed and then transformed into a swan, after which he was placed in the sky. The constellation of Cygnus is quite easy to spot as it is shaped like a cross. It is in fact sometimes known as the Northern Cross.

FESTIVAL FUN

If you found it hard to stick to your New Year's resolutions, you could try starting again in September! This month is a time for new beginnings for some religions. It is also time to give thanks for nature's gift to us of the harvest.

23rd September *Mabon or Harvest Festival*

The harvest festival is the closest thing we have to a day of thanksgiving in Britain. The word 'harvest' comes from the Old English word *hærfest* meaning 'autumn'. This was a very important time of year, as the success of the harvest could mean the difference between life or death for a whole community. In the past, even children had to help bring in the harvest. Then, as soon as it was over, everyone would return from the fields for the harvest supper. This was a huge feast with much singing and laughter.

25th September *Rosh Hashanah*

This is a very important Jewish festival as it celebrates the start of the New Year in the Hebrew calendar. It is one of Judaism's holiest days and begins the month of Tishri, which is the seventh month in the Hebrew calendar. Rosh Hashanah is a time for giving thanks for the birth of the universe and the day on which God created Adam and Eve. The festival begins at sunset on 25th September and goes through to sunset on 27th September. People light candles, enjoy special meals and come together to pray.

DID YOU KNOW...

Rosh Hashanah means 'Head of the Year'. Jewish people believe that the things we say and do during this time will control what happens for the rest of the year, just as our head controls our body.

29th September *Michaelmas Day*

The Christian celebration of Michaelmas, or the 'Feast of St Michael and All Angels' falls near the equinox. Traditionally, Michaelmas Day was the time when new servants were hired or land was bought or sold, and money was paid back to people who had lent it. This is why most schools and universities start their new year around September; some of them even call the autumn term 'Michaelmas Term'.

YOU SAY TOMATO...

Is the tomato a fruit or a vegetable? People have been arguing about this for hundreds of years: in America in 1887 the argument went all the way to the US Supreme Court! This sounds silly, but it was quite important because if it was decided that tomatoes were vegetables, they would be more expensive.

In actual fact, the tomato is a fruit because it contains seeds and grows on a vine. The same is true of cucumbers, squashes, beans and peas. But, of course, everyone thinks of them as vegetables because they are served in savoury dishes and not as desserts!

We can get tomatoes all year round, but when growing your own, the best time to pick them is often in late August or early September. While the days are still golden and warm, it's lovely to throw your own tomatoes into a salad. As the month wears on, you might be left with a few that are not so nice to eat raw, but they are great for soups, chutneys, stews and this delicious tomato sauce.

Recipe for *The Best Tomato Sauce Ever!*

This sauce is one of the easiest and most useful recipes you'll ever learn to make, as you can add it to so many things: pizza, chicken, curries, pasta – even soups.

You will need:

Sharp knife
Large bowl or saucepan
Kettle
Colander
Chopping board
Garlic crusher (optional)
Large frying pan
Wooden spoon
Pots for freezing (optional)

1 kg fresh tomatoes (or 2 x 400 g tins of chopped tomatoes)
1 large brown onion, finely chopped
1 tablespoon of vegetable oil
3 garlic cloves, finely chopped or crushed
1 handful of fresh basil, torn (or dried herbs such as oregano)
A few drops of Worcestershire sauce (leave out for vegetarians)
1 tablespoon of tomato ketchup
Salt and pepper to taste

1. *Make a small cut in the skin of each fresh tomato, then put them all into the large bowl. If you are using tinned tomatoes, start from step 5.*
2. *Ask an adult to help you boil a kettle and pour hot water over the tomatoes, leaving them to soak for 1–2 minutes. Then drain the tomatoes in a colander and return them to the bowl.*
3. *Pour cold water over the tomatoes, and leave for a minute before draining.*
4. *It should be easy to peel the skins off the tomatoes and chop them. Put them aside.*
5. *Fry the chopped onion in the oil on the hob on a gentle heat, stirring often with a wooden spoon until it is soft but not browned.*
6. *Add the chopped garlic and stir for a couple of minutes.*
7. *Add the chopped tomatoes and any juice (fresh or tinned) and stir.*
8. *Add half of the torn basil leaves, a few drops of Worcestershire sauce and a tablespoon of tomato ketchup.*
9. *Leave to simmer for at least an hour, or about half an hour if using tinned tomatoes. The sauce should become darker and thicker.*
10. *Add the rest of the ripped basil and salt and pepper to taste.*

IN THEIR FOOTSTEPS

Have you ever noticed any funny footprints in the mud or on pavements where you live? You might have found the tracks of an animal that has crept past your house at night when you were fast asleep!

Why not go on a tracking walk around the streets where you live and see what you can spot? Crazy as it may seem, it's a good idea to take a torch with you even in the day, as tracks can be hard to see in direct sunlight.

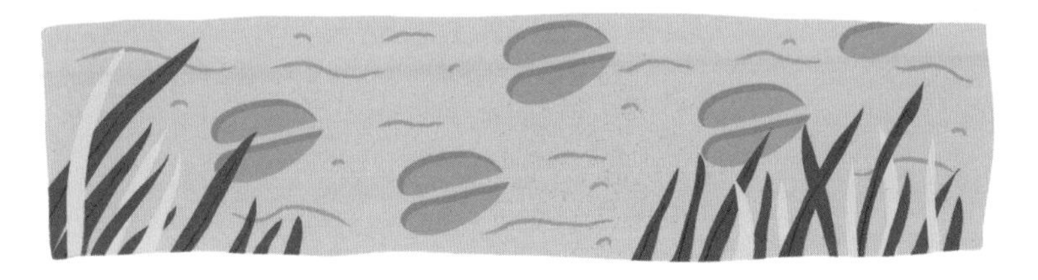

You could have a go at copying or tracing the prints on the opposite page. Put them on separate cards or pieces of paper and label them. Take the cards out on your walk, and when you spot a print that looks like one on your card, write where and when you saw it on the back.

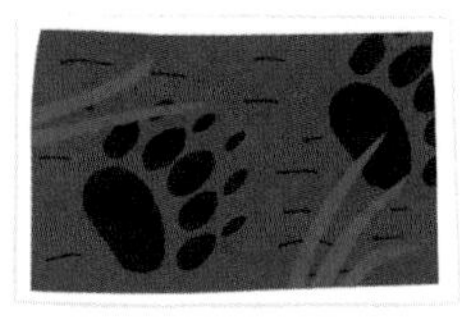

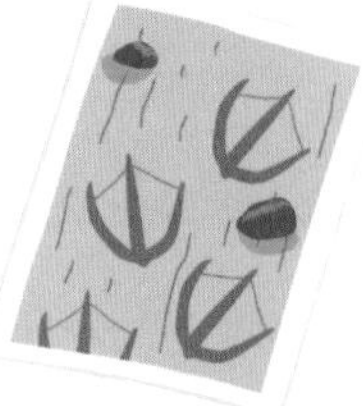

Look out for prints on walls and even on cars. See if you can notice other clues that an animal or bird has been nearby. Can you spot any scratch marks on trees? A squirrel, bird or cat might have made those. What about silvery snail and slug trails or spiders' webs or bird droppings?

It's not only animals that leave tracks – we humans do as well. Running barefoot is the best way to see how we leave our marks. If you live near the sea, go to the beach on a warm September day and take your shoes and socks off. Is it possible to tell if you were walking or running simply by looking at your tracks?

Animal Print Guide

BERRY GOOD FOR YOU!

Rosehips are the berries that form after the roses have wilted – you must leave the dead flowers on the rose bush if you want the hips, though. If you 'deadhead' your roses (i.e. remove the dead roses) you won't have any hips!

The hips come in all sizes and in a range of shades of red. They are filled with tiny seeds and covered with silky hairs, so if you follow the recipe to make the syrup, you'll need to strain the liquid through a muslin cloth to get rid of the hairs.

Rosehip syrup is like a cordial that you mix with water to make a tasty drink. As well as being delicious, it has been given as a natural remedy for centuries. It is believed to keep away coughs and colds in winter time.

Even if you don't have roses at home, you will be able to find wild rosebushes in the woods and hedgerows. You'll need to wear gloves to stop yourself from being scratched by the thorns on the rosebush. Make sure you pick only the ripest berries that are bright red and slightly soft – these will be the sweetest. As always with foraging wild food, make sure you have checked first that you are picking the right fruit, because some red berries from other plants can be poisonous.

Recipe for *Rosehip Syrup*

Fresh rosehips can also be used to make jelly, jam and pickles. You can even dry them and sprinkle them on cereal.

You will need:

Large saucepan
Kettle
Muslin cloth or jelly bag
Large bowl
Medium saucepan
Metal spoon
Sterilised jars or bottles

1 kg rosehips
2 l boiling water
1.5 l cold water
350 g caster sugar

TOP TIP

If you can't find as much as 1 kg rosehips, use a mixture of 500 g rosehips and 500 g blackberries.

1. *Put the rosehips in a large saucepan.*
2. *Ask an adult to help you pour 2 l of boiling water on to the hips.*
3. *Bring the mixture back to the boil, then turn off the heat and allow it to sit for 15 minutes so that the rosehips flavour the water.*
4. *Strain the mixture through a muslin cloth or jelly bag into a large bowl to get rid of any pulp or hairs on the berries, squeezing out as much liquid as you can, then set the bowl aside.*
5. *Tip the gooey berry mixture from the muslin cloth or jelly bag back into the saucepan.*
6. *Pour in 1.5 l of cold water and bring the mixture to the boil.*
7. *Turn off the heat and allow it to sit for 10 minutes.*
8. *Repeat the straining process through the muslin cloth or jelly bag.*
9. *Throw away the goo that is left in the muslin cloth or jelly bag.*
10. *Pour all the strained rosehip liquid into a medium saucepan and boil it rapidly until the amount of liquid left is reduced by half – to about 1 litre.*
11. *Use a metal spoon to skim off any scum that comes to the surface, then stir in the sugar until it is dissolved.*
12. *Pour the syrup into sterilised jars or bottles.*
13. *The syrup will keep for up to three months, stored in the fridge. If it is too sweet, dilute it with some tap water.*

BONKERS FOR CONKERS

'Conkers' is the name of a traditional game that is played using the seeds from the horse chestnut tree.

Prepare Your Conkers

1. *Choose two of the biggest, smoothest, roundest conkers you can find.*
2. *Ask an adult to make a hole through the centre of each one, either with a nail or a screwdriver, or even a drill.*
3. *Take two long pieces of string or garden twine – about 20 cm long – and thread a piece through the hole in each conker. Make sure you tie a knot in the bottom so that the conkers don't just slide off!*
4. *Find a friend and challenge them to a game . . .*

TOP TIP

When playing, hold the conker low, away from your face, and never flick or throw a conker near someone else's face.

How to Play

★ Stand opposite each other, holding the end of the string so that the conkers are hanging down.

★ Take it in turns to hit your conker against your opponent's.

★ The conker that breaks the other one gains a point.

WILD SEA, WILD ME

Believe it or not, September is the best month to go for a swim in the sea. This is because the water has been warming up over the summer and it is now as warm as it will be all year. If you do fancy a dip, take a grown-up with you and be careful to check the tides beforehand. Make sure you are swimming in a safe area where you can get in and out easily. Also take a good look at the waves first, as the sea can begin to get quite stormy and rough in September.

OCTOBER

SPECIAL DAYS

5th Yom Kippur (Jewish holiday)

8th Prophet's birthday (Muslim celebration)

21st Apple Day

24th Diwali

30th Daylight saving ends

31st Samhain Eve (pagan festival)/All Saints' Eve (Christian festival)/Halloween

ANNIVERSARIES

65 years ago . . .

On 4 October 1957, Sputnik 1 was launched. It was the first human-made (not natural) satellite to orbit the Earth.

100 years ago . . .

George Cadbury died on 24 October 1922. He founded Cadbury's chocolate company in Birmingham and the town of Bournville, where he built houses for his workers.

100 years ago . . .

On 18 October 1922, the BBC was officially founded.

"I'm so glad I live in a world where there are Octobers."

L. M. MONTGOMERY (1874–1942)

October leads us gently into autumn. The days are still mild and the light is golden as it reflects off the turning leaves. The colours are glorious! This is the perfect time of year to go out walking in the countryside and parks. Run through the fallen leaves and look out for especially beautiful colours and shapes. Maybe you could collect your favourite leaves and press them? Pressed autumn leaves make brilliant decorations on cards or bookmarks.

DID YOU KNOW...

Every October, servants and farm labourers used to go to the centre of their town or village to look for work, carrying something to show what job they did. Maids would carry a small mop, and so these gatherings became known as mop fairs. Nowadays, mop fairs are funfairs.

Why is October Called October?

October gets its name from the Latin word *octo* which means 'eight', and was named by the Romans during a time when the calendar year began with March instead of with January as it does now.

The Anglo-Saxon name for this month was *Winterfylleth* which comes from the words for winter and the full moon.

October Birth Signs

Libra is the birth sign for people born between 23rd September and 23rd October. Librans are said to have a balanced personality, so the sign looks like old-fashioned weighing scales. Librans are supposed to like peace and harmony.

Scorpio is the birth sign for people born between 24th October and 21st November. They are thought to be brave, passionate and stubborn! They are also said to like the truth and have deep, long-lasting friendships.

The Moon's a Balloon!

The October full moon is called the Hunter's Moon. It is also known as the Blood Moon because it can often be a striking red or orange colour. Of course, the colour of the actual moon hasn't changed! The moon hangs lower in the sky at this time of year, closer to the horizon, and so we are seeing it through more of the Earth's atmosphere. The gases around the Earth and the tiny particles in the air affect the way in which we see light. Orange and red light has longer wavelengths and so these are the colours we see reflected off the moon when it is closer to us.

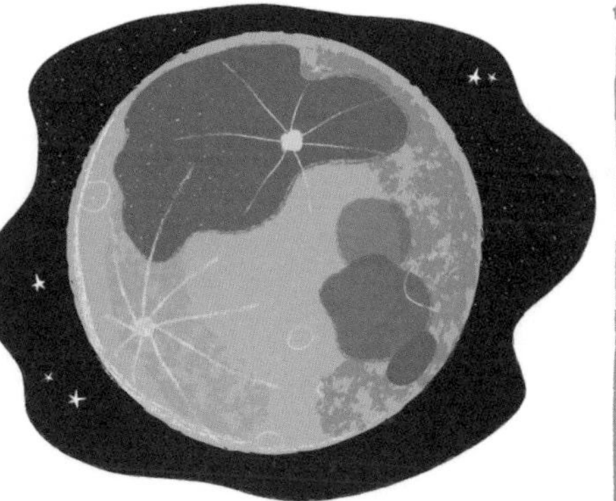

5th October *Yom Kippur*

This is the holiest day of the year for Jewish people. It is a day for saying sorry for things you have done wrong and asking for forgiveness. Jewish people traditionally wear white and they fast and pray for up to 25 hours. They often spend most of the day in the synagogue.

8th October *Prophet's Birthday*

In the UK and all over the world, some Muslims see this as a day to celebrate. In some countries there are street parades, the mosques are decorated and children read out poems about the Prophet's life. People can spend the day donating food and money to charity, too. Other Muslims see this day as a time for concentrating on the holy book, the *Qur'an*.

24th October *Diwali*

Diwali marks the start of the Hindu New Year. Sikhs and Jains also celebrate at this time. Diwali is five days long, and on the third day, many Hindus light special oil lamps called *diyas*. The lamps symbolise the triumph of light over darkness, good over evil and knowledge over ignorance. Many gods, including Rama and his wife, Sita, and Lakshmi, the goddess of wealth and prosperity, are celebrated with music, *puja* (prayers), firework displays and by sharing traditional sweets.

31st October *All Saints' Eve*

This is a Christian festival also known as All Hallows' Eve, Hallowed Evening or Holy Evening, which is how we get the name Halloween! On the evening of 31st October, some Christians begin three days of ceremonies and services to remember loved ones who have died and the saints ('hallowed' or holy people). It is traditional to light candles for those who have died and to spend time praying and remembering them.

31st October *Halloween*

Nowadays, we associate Halloween with fun and games and dressing-up. But in fact, as far back as the 16th century, people had parties on 31st October, playing games and practising rituals to try and tell the future, especially about deaths or marriages in the family. This is where the game of apple-bobbing comes from. It used to be thought that the first person to bite into an apple would be the first person to get married!

Before pumpkins were brought over from America, people would use turnips or other root vegetables to make lanterns. These were carved with ugly faces in the hope that they would scare away evil spirits.

PUMPKIN CARVING

How about carving your own lantern? These look great as table decorations for a Halloween party or you can leave them outside your house to welcome trick-or-treaters.

How scary can you make your pumpkin lantern? Draw the most monstrous face you can think of and then ask an adult to help you carve out the shapes!

You will need:

Medium-sized pumpkin
Chopping board
Large metal spoon
Medium bowl
Biro or marker pen
Sharp knife
Tealight

1. *Ask an adult to help you cut a small 'lid' off the top of your pumpkin.*
2. *Use the metal spoon to remove the seeds and scoop out as much of the flesh as you can.*
3. *Put the flesh in a bowl and put aside.*
4. *Draw a face on your pumpkin.*
5. *Ask an adult to help you cut out the eyes, nose and mouth.*
6. *Ask an adult to help you light a tealight and put it in your pumpkin.*
7. *Ask an adult to help you place your pumpkin in a safe position. Turn out all the lights! Your super scary pumpkin lantern is spookily ready for Halloween!*

Recipe for *Pumpkin Gingerbread*

This is a tasty way to use up all the pumpkin flesh that you have to scoop out before you can carve it into a pumpkin lantern.

You will need:

900 g loaf tin
Greaseproof paper
2 microwave-proof bowls
Potato masher
Sieve
Large mixing bowl
Wooden spoon
Food processor (optional)
Whisk
Metal skewer
Wire rack

Butter for greasing
250 g pumpkin flesh, roughly chopped
50 g black treacle
140 g golden syrup
140 g light brown soft sugar
100 ml semi-skimmed milk
225 g self-raising flour
1 teaspoon of bicarbonate of soda
1 tablespoon of ground ginger
2 teaspoons of allspice
Pinch of salt
100 g cold butter, diced
2 medium eggs, beaten
10 chunks of crystallised stem ginger, finely chopped

1. *Heat the oven to 180°C/160°C fan/ Gas Mark 4.*
2. *Grease and line the loaf tin with greaseproof paper.*
3. *Put the pumpkin flesh into a microwave-proof bowl.*
4. *Cook on a high heat in the microwave for 5–10 minutes, until the pumpkin is soft.*
5. *Drain off any liquid and mash the flesh with a potato masher or fork.*
6. *Measure the treacle, syrup, sugar and milk into another microwave-proof bowl and heat it for about 2 minutes until the sugar has dissolved.*
7. *Sieve the flour, bicarbonate of soda, spices and a pinch of salt into the food processor.*
8. *Tip in the diced butter and whizz everything together until no big lumps remain.*
9. *Whisk the mashed pumpkin and the egg into the sugar mixture.*
10. *Stir the wet ingredients into the dry ingredients to make a batter.*
11. *Pour into the loaf tin and scatter most of the crystallised ginger on top.*
12. *Bake for 45 minutes until a skewer poked into the centre comes out with moist crumbs attached.*
13. *Scatter over the remaining ginger, then cool the cake in the tin on a wire rack.*

BLACK HISTORY MONTH

Black History Month is in October in Britain. It's when people celebrate the contributions that black people have made to the country. The idea for Black History Month originally came from the USA and it is still celebrated there in February every year.

The American historian Carter G. Woodson came up with the idea. He had found that Americans knew a lot about the history of white people in their country, but that no one seemed to speak or write about the history of Black Americans. He wanted people to be properly educated so that Black people would no longer be discriminated against and treated badly because of the colour of their skin, so he set up the Association for the Study of Negro Life and History in 1915 which encouraged historians to research and write about Black history and culture.

Ignatius Sancho

Mary Prince

In the 1970s, a man called Akyaaba Addai-Sebo went from Britain to America and was inspired by Black History Month. He thought that Britain should be celebrating it, too, so he started the British version in 1987.

Black History Month is a time for celebration and remembrance, and there are many wonderful talks, food festivals and musical events you can go to – everything that celebrates the achievements, culture and contributions from Black people to our lives today.

DID YOU KNOW...

It is believed that Black History Month is celebrated in October in Britain because, traditionally, October is when African chiefs and leaders gather to settle their differences, so Akyaaba chose this month to reconnect with African roots.

Mary Seacole

Rosa Parks

Martin Luther King Jr.

APPLES GALORE

October is apple month! If you live in an area where there are a lot of apple trees, you might find lots of apples falling into the street. These are known as 'windfalls'. They might look battered and bruised, but windfalls are excellent apples to put in pies, crumbles and cakes. They make delicious apple sauce as well, which is yummy as a dessert with ice cream or yoghurt and also goes very well with roast pork. Always check windfalls carefully as there are a lot of sleepy wasps around at this time of year and they can sometimes be found slowly munching their way through apples that have fallen to the ground. You will also need to wash windfalls and cut out any bruised flesh before you use them for cooking.

Apple Day takes place on 21st October to celebrate apples and orchards!

Recipe for *Easy Peasy Apple Tart*

You will need:

Baking tray
Greaseproof paper
Sharp knife
Glass bowl
Lemon squeezer
Pastry brush

375 g packet of rolled puff pastry
5 large eating apples such as Cox's or Russets
Juice of 1 lemon
25 g butter, melted
1 teaspoon of vanilla extract
1 tablespoon of caster sugar
3 tablespoons of apricot jam

The lemon juice stops the apples from going brown!

1. *Heat the oven to 220°C/200°C fan/Gas Mark 7.*
2. *Put the pastry on a baking tray lined with greaseproof paper.*
3. *Peel, core and thinly slice the apples and lightly toss them in a glass bowl with the lemon juice.*
4. *Arrange the apple slices over the pastry but leave 2 cm of pastry showing at the edges.*
5. *Melt the butter on the hob or in the microwave and mix in the vanilla extract.*
6. *Pour this mixture on to the apples.*
7. *Sprinkle the tart with caster sugar.*
8. *Bake for 15–20 minutes until the apples are tender and the pastry is crisp.*
9. *Melt the jam on a gentle heat and then brush it over the apples.*
10. *Serve warm with vanilla ice cream for a yummy autumnal dessert!*

Make a *Scary Scarecrow*

Scarecrows were first made as a way to stop birds from eating farmers' crops. Figures were made from wood and straw and then placed in fields against poles.

These days, people use many materials to make scarecrows: pots, clothes, straw, wood, clay, tins and paint. Why not make your own scarecrow? Put it in the window at Halloween to make trick-or-treaters jump! Remember to ask your parents or carers before taking any of the things you'll need to make your scarecrow.

You will need:

3 bamboo canes or strong sticks (2 m, 1 m and 30 cm long)
String
Old pair of tights
Straw, old newspapers or leaves
Paint or permanent markers
Old clothes
Old hat

1. *Make a frame for your scarecrow by tying the 1 m cane or stick tightly to the 2 m cane or stick with string about 15 cm from one end, in a cross shape.*
2. *Tie the 30 cm cane or stick in the same way about halfway down.*
3. *Take one leg of the tights and stuff it with straw, newspaper or leaves. Push the stuffing to the foot end and mould it into a head shape.*
4. *Knot the leg of the tights around the bottom of the head to stop the straw from falling out.*
5. *Draw or paint a funny or scary face on it.*
6. *Now tie the head on to the top of the frame with string.*
7. *Dress your scarecrow! You could put a shirt on the top crossbar and the trousers on the smaller bar, for example.*
8. *Tie off the bottom of the trouser legs with string and stuff them as you did the head.*
9. *Button up the shirt and tie the ends of the arms, then stuff the sleeves.*
10. *Push some straw under the hat and leave it sticking out to look like hair!*

THE DARK IS RISING

The days are getting shorter and shorter. However, we still have light evenings until the clocks change on 30th October. This means we get an extra hour in bed the night before. It can be confusing if you are a baby or a pet as it messes around with your mealtimes!

Why Do the Clocks Change?

We didn't always bother with changing the clocks. In the old days, people went to bed when the sun went down and got up again when it rose. Midday was several minutes earlier in the east of the country than it was in the south, and several minutes later in the west. This meant that town clocks across the British Isles showed different times. The building of the railway network changed all that because the time had to be the same all over the country, or people would not have had the faintest idea when to catch a train.

Then a man called William Willett suggested to parliament that if the clocks changed, we would all enjoy more daylight in the autumn and winter months. So, since 1916, the clocks have gone back one hour in October and in March the clocks have been put forward by one hour. This is known as 'daylight saving'.

TOP TIP

In spring, the clocks spring forward an hour, and in the autumn, they fall back.

NOVEMBER

SPECIAL DAYS

1st All Saints' Day (Christian celebration)
2nd All Souls' Day (Christian celebration)
5th Guy Fawkes Night (Bonfire Night)
11th Armistice Day (Remembrance Day)/Martinmas
13th Remembrance Sunday
20th Stir-up Sunday (last Sunday before Advent)
27th First Sunday of Advent (Christian celebration)
30th St Andrew's Day (Scotland)

ANNIVERSARIES

100 years ago . . .

On 4 November 1922, the British archaeologist Howard Carter discovered the tomb of the Egyptian pharaoh Tutankhamun.

100 years ago . . .

On 26 November 1922, the cartoonist Charles Schulz was born. He is famous for inventing the Peanuts gang, featuring Snoopy, Charlie Brown and Woodstock.

150 years ago . . .

On 7 November 1872, the *Mary Celeste* set sail from New York on a voyage to Italy. The ship is famous for being found abandoned with no crew left on board. Many stories have been told about this 'ghost ship'!

"November's sky
is chill
and drear."

We can no longer deny it – winter is on its way! The shortest day is less than two months' away, so it is no wonder that so many festivals this month celebrate light. Many festivals also focus on sweet-tasting food – a sweet treat can be just what you need when you've been outside, battling the cold! There is also all the fun of Bonfire Night to look forward to.

If your family and friends are having a bonfire for Bonfire Night, make sure you protect any curious hedgehogs who might try and burrow their way into the piles of leaves and wood. You can stop hedgehogs from doing this by building a small fence with chicken wire around the edge. And if you do find a hedgehog, put on some gardening gloves (or oven gloves) before touching its spiky little body. This is also to protect the hedgehog as they don't like getting the smell of humans on them!

Constellation of the Month

Taurus is the Latin word for 'bull'. Look out for this constellation in the east, where it starts the night low in the sky. If you look for the bright orange giant star called Aldebaran, that will help you find the rest of the constellation.

DID YOU KNOW...

In some parts of the country, 4th November is known as Mischief Night. People play tricks on one another, mainly by hiding belongings or putting them in the wrong place!

Why is November Called November?

The word 'November' comes from the Latin word for the number nine, *novem*. This is because, just like September and October before it, November keeps its name from a time when the calendar had only 10 months.

The Anglo-Saxons called this month *Blotmonath,* which means 'blood month'. This is because it was traditional at this time of year to kill farm animals and preserve the meat for the winter months ahead.

FESTIVAL FUN

5th November *Guy Fawkes or Bonfire Night*

"Remember, remember the 5th of November, Gunpowder, treason and plot!"

This is an annual commemoration of the day in 1605 when a man called Guy Fawkes was arrested for being a part of the 'Gunpowder Plot'. The plot was thought up by a group of men who wanted to blow up King James I and the Houses of Parliament in London. Guy Fawkes was found hiding beneath the House of Lords, guarding some explosives. Thankfully, the bombs never went off.

Nowadays, people spend the evening going to firework displays, standing around a big bonfire and eating hot dogs! It is a great way to chase away the winter blues.

11th November *Armistice Day (Remembrance Day)*

Armistice Day or Remembrance Day is a time for remembering all those who were killed in the First and Second World Wars and other wars that have since followed. A two-minute silence is held to remember the dead on the Sunday nearest to 11th November. People traditionally wear a red poppy around this time to show that they have not forgotten the people who died in the war.

20th November *Stir-up Sunday*

This is the last Sunday before Advent, which is the period of time in which Christians prepare for Christmas, and is the day people traditionally make their Christmas puddings. In the old days, it was a time for families to get together to mix and steam the pudding. Everyone would take a turn to stir the pudding and make a special wish for the year ahead.

27th November *First Sunday of Advent*

Advent lasts for four Sundays leading up to Christmas. Advent always begins on the Sunday that falls between 27th November and 3rd December. In churches, Christians light one candle every Sunday of Advent. It is common for people to also begin their own countdown to Christmas on 1st December with Advent calendars or Advent candles which have the numbers 1 to 24 on them.

CELEBRATE AUTUMN!

Confetti is fun to throw in the air at celebrations or to put inside balloons or a piñata for parties. However, most confetti is made of plastic or paper which then causes litter and pollution, so some people are choosing not to use it any more.

If you still like the idea of using confetti, don't worry! You can make your own beautiful multi-coloured confetti which is perfectly safe for the environment and also great fun to make. It will keep for months if you put it in a Tupperware pot or any box with a lid. And when it falls to the ground outside, it doesn't matter because it will biodegrade into the earth and help to make lovely soil for plants to grow in when the spring comes again!

How to make *Leaf Confetti*

You will need:

Lots of autumn leaves
Old newspaper
Large, heavy book or a flower press
Hole punch
Pot with a lid

1. *Collect as many beautiful fallen autumn leaves in as many different colours as you can.*
2. *To dry and flatten the leaves, first put them between sheets of newspaper and then put these between the pages of a large book or use a flower press if you have one.*
3. *Using a hole punch, cut holes from the flattened leaves.*
4. *Empty the hole punch and put all the little circles in a pot with a lid.*
5. *Save them for a party or celebration!*

TOP TIP

You can use the leaves with holes in to make cards – you could even save them until next month to make Christmas cards!

BE A BEETLE DETECTIVE

You might think there isn't much to see outside this month. However, if you look down and look closely, you'll see there's a whole mini world beneath your feet, beetling about in the undergrowth! Beetles are easy to recognise because their front wings look like hard shells which cover their second pair of wings. Remember to ask an adult before you go digging around in flower beds, and always return the beetles to the soil where you found them and wash your hands afterwards.

You will need:

Pots with see-through plastic lids
Skewer
Paper or card
Magnifying glass
Pencil and/or coloured crayons

1 *Prepare the pots for the insects by making breathing holes in the lids. Ask an adult to help you do this with a skewer.*

2 *Go and hunt for beetles! Look in gardens, parks, woods or even in plant pots on windowsills. They like to hide in cool, damp places. Move stones and look closely at flowers, leaves, tree stumps and soil.*

3 *Collect any beetles you find by carefully using a piece of paper or card to pick them up.*

4 *Put the beetles in the pots. (Try not to mix up different sorts of beetle, just in case they try to eat each other!)*

5 *Have a look at the beetles using your magnifying glass.*

6 *If it's easier to see, put the beetles on a clean piece of paper to examine them.*

7 *Draw a picture of them if you like and label them if you know what they are.*

8 *Ask yourself: how many legs do they have? What colours are they? Do they have any patterns on them? What do their faces look like? How do they defend themselves?*

BRILLIANT BEETLES

There are more types of beetle than any other type of insect. In Britain there are about 4,000 species, and they make up 40 per cent of insect life in this country. It is thought that there are around 350,000 beetle species worldwide.

CAN YOU SPOT...

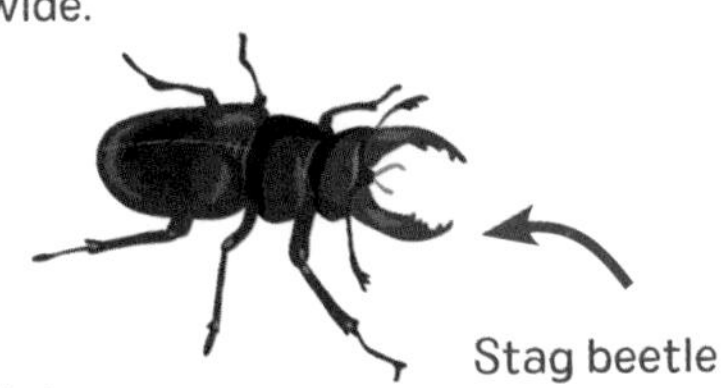

7-spot ladybird

This is one of the most familiar beetles and you have probably seen a lot of them. They are very useful to gardeners as they like to eat greenfly (also known as aphids).

Stag beetle

This is Britain's largest beetle, but you may never see one as it spends most of its life below ground feeding on dead wood. Male stag beetles have 'antlers' which are actually large jaws.

Green tiger beetle

This scary looking minibeast has long legs and sharp jaws. It takes short flying leaps to attack its prey or to escape danger.

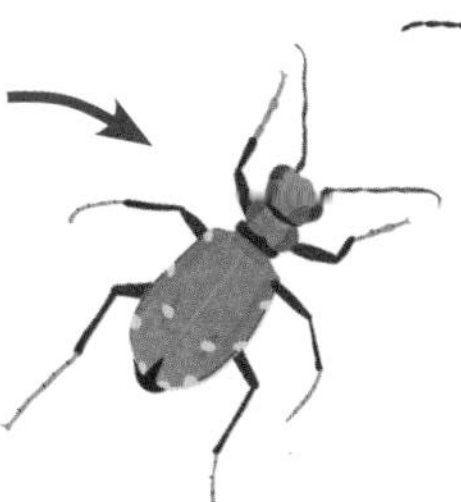

Violet ground beetle

This beetle is large and moves very fast. It goes out mainly at night and can be found in woods, meadows and gardens. If it is frightened, it gives off a nasty smell.

Cockchafer

This beetle is mostly nocturnal. Sometimes it is known as the May bug because it comes out in the spring.

Devil's coach-horse

This large beetle looks like a mini monster! It likes damp places so will mostly be found under logs and stones. It can give you a nasty nip, so be careful.

Oil beetle

These large insects get their name from the oils they release. They are usually found in the spring on meadow flowers.

PRETTY PEBBLES

Whenever you pick up a pebble on a beach, you are holding the story of Planet Earth in your hand! Pebbles begin as chunks of rock that break off from cliffs, or are brought down to the sea by rivers. Some of them come from man-made things such as glass. Pebbles are formed by the way they are bashed about as they fall or the way they are worn smooth by water. Some of them have shiny flecks that glint in the sun. Some are dark and dense. When they are wet, you may see strange and wonderful textures and patterns inside them.

DID YOU KNOW...

A pebble is a stone that is no larger than a tennis ball and no smaller than a pea. Anything bigger is a stone or rock and anything smaller is gravel, shingle or sand.

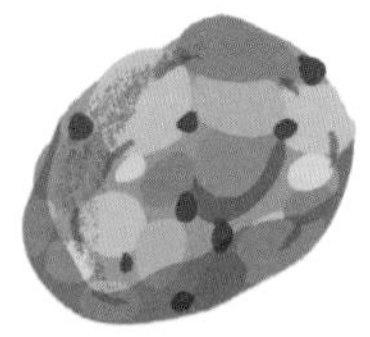
Conglomerate

Sea glass

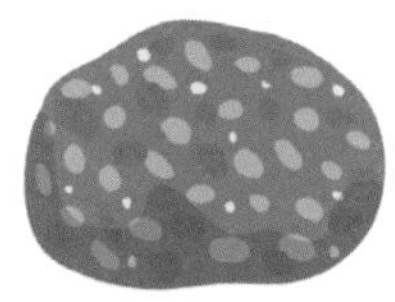
Spotted slate

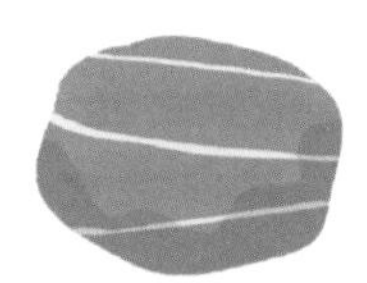
Quartz veinstone

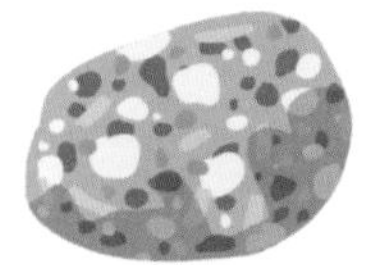
Granite

Sandstone

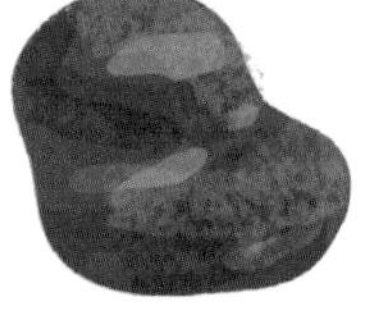
Serpentine

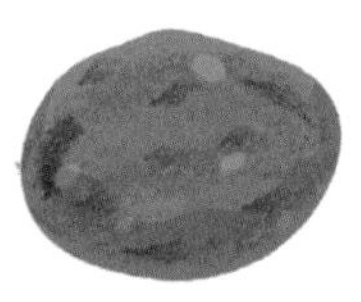
Schist

Jasper

Flint

Quartz breccia

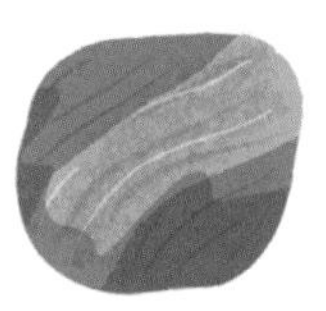
Pink feldspar veins

SEE THE SEALS

There are two types of seal found around the British coast: the common seal and the grey seal. The common seal gives birth to pups in the summer, whereas the grey seal has its pups in November. The grey seal spends a lot of time in the sea, where it hunts for fish, squid, crab and lobster. They live in large family groups called 'colonies' which can be made up of thousands of seals.

★ The grey seal prefers the rocky coasts found in northern and western parts of the country and is most likely to be seen off the coast of Northumberland, Lincolnshire, the Orkney Islands and Cornwall.

★ The grey seal grows to a much larger size than the common seal and males are much bigger than females.

★ The grey seal has a much longer nose or 'snout' than the common seal and has nostrils spaced further apart!

★ Seals like to leave the water to rest and bask in the sun after they have been hunting.

Grey seal

Common seal

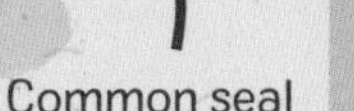

THE COLOURS OF NATURE

Sometimes during winter walks the weather is not great and you are trudging along in the mud, wishing you were tucked up snug indoors instead. A good idea to make walks more fun is to play games on your way. See if you can get the grown-ups to join in! You are bound to be faster than they are . . .

This is a fun activity to do on a winter walk. You might think that there are not many colours around at this time of the year – after all, there are fewer flowers around now and most of the autumn leaves have fallen from the trees. It might look quite bleak and bare outside – all brown and grey and boring.

Is it, though? Next time you go for a walk, try this activity. It might change your mind about how boring the natural world looks in winter! You can either complete the activity outside or, if it's a chilly day, bring your treasures home to finish.

You will need:

Paint chart (free of charge from most DIY stores)
Bag or large pockets!

1 *Look out for any small items you can find: sticks, stones, nut shells, leaves, wild seed heads, feathers, bark and pine cones.*

2 *Put these items carefully in your bag or pockets.*

3 *Once you think you have enough items, find a sheltered place to stop.*

4 *Lay the colour chart out on the ground or on a picnic table.*

5 *Lay the items you have found next to the chart.*

6 *Look carefully at the chart – can you match your items to the colours on it?*

7 *How many different browns, greens, greys, yellows, reds and oranges have you found? Have you found any other colours?*

DECEMBER

SPECIAL DAYS

18th Hanukkah begins

21st Winter solstice/Midwinter/Yule (pagan celebration)/Start of winter

24th Christmas Eve/First day of Christmas (Christian celebration)

25th Christmas Day (Christian celebration)

26th Boxing Day/Last day of Hanukkah

31st New Year's Eve/Hogmanay (Scotland)

ANNIVERSARIES

85 years ago . . .

On 21 December 1937, Disney showed *Snow White and the Seven Dwarfs* for the first time. It was the first full-length Disney cartoon movie.

200 years ago . . .

On 27 December 1822, the French chemist and biologist Louis Pasteur was born. He is known for his work on vaccinations and also for developing 'pasteurisation' which is a way of preserving milk and wine.

"I heard a bird sing In the dark of December."

OLIVER HERFORD (1863–1935)

For many of us, December means only one thing – Christmas! However, it's not the only festival being celebrated this month. There have always been lots of festivities in December because we are heading towards the shortest day of the year, or Midwinter. Try and make the most of the daylight this month. Which birds can you hear singing at dawn? Are the owls busy near you at dusk? Can you spot squirrels trying to find the nuts they buried in the early autumn? It's not only humans that are busy preparing food and gathering supplies at this time of year!

December may be the start of winter, but by the end of the month the days are already getting longer. It is because of this promise of longer, lighter days that the longest night has traditionally been a time for celebration. The dark can be sad or scary sometimes, but just think: if there was no darkness, there would be no light! This is what all the festivals this month are about: finding light in the darkness.

The one thing you may hope for and not get this month is snow. You are far more likely to get snow from February through to March in Britain.

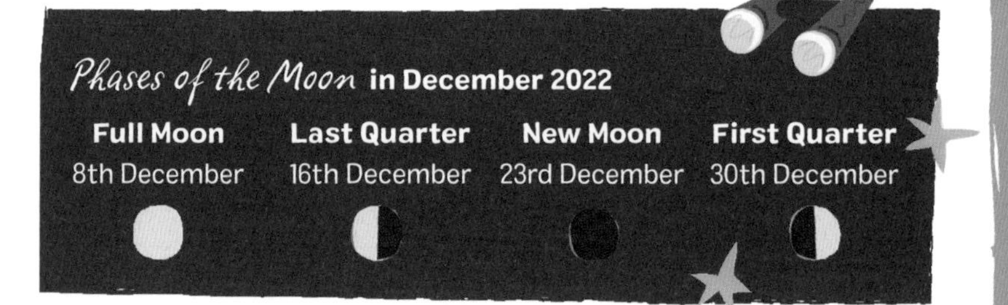

Phases of the Moon **in December 2022**

Full Moon	Last Quarter	New Moon	First Quarter
8th December	16th December	23rd December	30th December

Why is December Called December?

This month gets its name from the Latin word for tenth, *decem*. The Anglo-Saxons called December *Ærra Geola* or the month 'before Yule'. Yule was an important winter festival and is still celebrated today by pagans. Many of the 'Yuletide' traditions have found their way into things we now think of as Christmas traditions.

December Birth Signs

Sagittarius is represented by a centaur – a mythological creature who is half-man, half-horse. People born under the sign of Sagittarius, on or between 22nd November and 21st December, are supposed to be generous and have a great sense of humour. They can also be very impatient and will often speak first and think after!

Capricorn is the tenth birth sign and is represented by a goat with large horns and a fishtail. This is because, in legend, Capricorn was a sea-goat. The dates for this sign are 22nd December to 19th January. People born under this sign are thought to be ambitious and disciplined, but they can also be worriers.

DID YOU KNOW...

There is an old saying that "a clear, star-filled sky on Christmas Eve will bring good crops in the summer".

FESTIVAL FUN

There's so much festival fun this month, you could be forgiven for thinking that December is one long celebration from start to finish!

18th December *Hanukkah Begins*

Sometimes spelled *Chanukah*, this Jewish festival lasts for eight days. During this time, Jewish people remember how the Second Temple in Jerusalem was dedicated to God. Hanukkah is often called the festival of lights because the holiday is celebrated with the lighting of the *menorah* candlestick. Traditional foods are served, such as potato pancakes and jam-filled doughnuts called *sufganiyot*.

21st December *Winter solstice or Midwinter or Yule*

The winter solstice or Midwinter falls on the shortest day of the year and has been celebrated in Britain for hundreds of years. Many pagan traditions of Yule have found their way into the celebration of Christmas. At Yule, pagans light candles and fires, decorate their homes with evergreen plants, feast, dance and give gifts. All these things are now traditional at Christmas, too.

Pagans also believe that hanging a sprig of holly near the door brings good luck and keeps away evil spirits. Mistletoe is also hung as a decoration and as a blessing and symbol of new life.

Five ways to *Celebrate Midwinter*

★ Go on a walk to gather greenery for your home.
★ Light a fire or a circle of candles.
★ Tell stories around the fire or by candlelight.
★ Have a feast with your favourite food and favourite family and friends!
★ Write down a list of everything you have to be thankful for in the past year.

OUT IN THE WILD

While we humans are busy huddling by the fire and staying warm and cosy, nature carries on working. If you have had enough of being stuck indoors, get your family out on a nature walk. Wrap up warm and keep your eyes peeled. It might be winter, but there's still lots to see!

Robins are very busy at this time of year singing to protect their territories and finding food.

Listen out as the sun goes down and you might hear tawny owls calling to one another. The female calls out, "Too-wit," and the male answers her, "Too-whoo!"

Go for a walk around a river estuary. Birds flock to these places in the winter as the water does not freeze so there is always a lot of food to be found. You might even see a kingfisher or an otter.

Foxes are out hunting in the early evening. They can often be seen slinking into hedges or scurrying down driveways just after the sun has set.

Go for a walk by the sea. This is a great time of year to search the empty beaches for treasures – strange twisted lumps of driftwood, shells, pebbles and seed pods can all be used to make beautiful decorations.

Walk in the woods, too! Collect holly and ivy and pine cones and twigs and then come home and have fun making natural decorations for the house.

The tradition of hanging a wreath on the door goes back a long way. The Romans hung them as signs of victory and rich Roman women wore them as headdresses. Today's Christmas wreaths come from the German tradition of making Advent wreaths to celebrate the lead up to Christmas.

You can make your own wreath easily from things you find outside. Remember to wear gloves while gathering what you need and while making your wreath.

Make a *Winter Wreath*

You will need:

Gardening gloves
Moss
Wreath ring (you can buy one from a florist)
Green garden string
Scissors
Small conifer branches
Ivy leaves and berries
Dried leaves
Herbs such as sage or rosemary
Cinnamon sticks
Floristry wire
Fir cones
Dried clementines or orange slices
A wide piece of ribbon – red, gold or silver works well

1. *Stuff lots and lots of moss into the wreath ring until it is tightly packed.*
2. *Fix the moss in place using the green string.*
3. *Make a loop of the string on the back of the frame for hanging later.*
4. *Take small bunches of the branches, leaves, berries and herbs, mixing them up as you go.*
5. *Attach these bunches to the moss using the green string. Overlap them to avoid gaps and continue until all your moss is covered.*
6. *Stand back and look at the wreath to make sure you have kept a good circular shape and to check for gaps.*
7. *Tie cinnamon sticks together with the floristry wire and then use more wire to tie them on to the wreath. Do the same with the pine cones and the dried clementines or orange slices, too.*
8. *Tie the ribbon into a bow and attach it to the wreath at the bottom using the string or wire.*

CHRISTMAS TABLE DECORATIONS

Why not make some homemade Christmas decorations? It's a great thing to do at the beginning of the Christmas holidays when you are trying to pass the time, counting down to Christmas Day – and it's a lot cheaper than buying some! It's always nice to make the dinner table look lovely on Christmas Day. How about making Santa or elf place settings for everyone who is invited?

Make a *Festive Place Setting*

You will need:

Loo rolls or cardboard rolls
Red paper
Green paper
PVA glue
Pompoms in various colours
Black felt-tip pen
Cotton wool
White paper or white sticky labels

1. *If you are using cardboard rolls instead of loo rolls, cut them to size. They should be about 10 cm high.*
2. *Cover the roll in red paper for Santa, or green for the elves.*
3. *Use glue to fix the paper in place.*
4. *Use the pompoms to make buttons and noses.*
5. *Use the black felt-tip pen to draw on the eyes and any other features.*
6. *Use cotton wool for Santa's beard and the fur trim on his red coat. You can give the elves beards, too, if you like. Leave some space on their tummies for the next step.*
7. *Write your guests' or relatives' names on the white paper or sticky labels.*
8. *Stick these on the tummy area of each of the figures you have made.*
9. *Decide where everyone is going to sit and put the place settings out so that people can find their place at the table!*

25th December *Christmas Day*

The word Christmas comes from the Anglo-Saxon words *Cristes Mæsse*. It is the Christian celebration of the birth of Jesus Christ. In fact, his birth date is unknown. However, Christians wanted a day to celebrate their belief that Jesus brought goodness and light into the world. As there were already 'light festivals' at this time of year, such as Yule, it made sense to have Christmas then as well.

Saturnalia is an ancient Roman festival that probably influenced how and when Christmas is celebrated. It was dedicated to the god Saturn. All work and business stopped during the festival, and slaves were given a few days of freedom. People said *"Lo Saturnalia!"* to each other the way people today might say "Happy Christmas!" or "Happy Hanukkah!" At the end of the festival people would make presents of candles to one another or wax models of fruit.

31st December *New Year's Eve or Hogmanay*

It is the last day of the year! Just before midnight, it is traditional to turn on a radio or television to follow the countdown of the last few minutes of the old year and to watch the display of fireworks over the River Thames in London. At this point, people often hug and kiss and start to sing the song 'Auld Lang Syne' – although they often don't know the words! Here they are so that you can sing them this year:

"Should auld acquaintance be forgot,
and never brought to mind?
Should auld acquaintance be forgot
and auld lang syne?
For auld lang syne my dear,
for auld lang syne.
We'll tak'a cup o' kindness yet,
for auld lang syne."

The words were written by the Scottish poet Robert Burns in 1788. The song asks if it's right to forget old friends and things that have happened in the past.

DID YOU KNOW . . .

In England and Scotland, New Year's Day used to be 25th March. Scotland made 1st January New Year's Day in 1660 and England followed in 1752.

Just After Midnight . . .

In Scotland, New Year's Eve is known as Hogmanay. If you're lucky enough to be in Scotland on 31st December (and you're allowed to stay up on New Year's Eve until after midnight!) you might be able to join in with the tradition of first-footing.

The 'first foot' to come in through the front door after the last stroke of midnight is supposed to bring good luck. The 'first-footer' should be carrying a piece of coal, some bread, salt and a small drink (known as a 'wee dram'). These items are thought to bring warmth, good food, long life and good cheer for the year ahead.

Recipe for *Christmas Cranberry Jam*

It's always fun to make things for Christmas, and it's especially nice to make homemade presents. Why not have a go at this very easy cranberry jam recipe? This jam can be used instead of cranberry sauce to eat with turkey after Christmas and is also delicious on toast or crumpets for a Christmassy breakfast or snack. You can also make jam tarts with it!

You will need:

Large saucepan
Wooden spoon
Metal spoon
Sterilised jars
Waxed paper discs

225 g fresh or defrosted cranberries
225 g caster sugar
Zest of one orange

1. *Heat the cranberries and sugar over a low heat for about 10–15 minutes until the sugar dissolves and the cranberries begin to pop.*
2. *Add the orange zest and stir in.*
3. *Ask a grown-up to help you turn up the heat and boil the mixture rapidly for about 7 minutes.*
4. *Do the 'wrinkle test' to check that the jam has set.*
5. *Take off the heat and put into sterilised jars with a waxed paper disc on top of each one.*

The 'wrinkle test' involves dropping a teaspoon of jam on to a plate that you have put in the freezer before starting to make the jam. The hot jam hits the freezing surface and if it has set, it will wrinkle when you push it gently with your finger.

VISIT A LONELY NEIGHBOUR

Christmas is fun if you have everyone you love around the table and can enjoy playing games and spending a cosy time together. However, some people are not so fond of this time of year and can end up feeling very lonely while everyone else is gathering to celebrate.

Maybe you know someone who lives on their own and might appreciate a visit this Christmas? You could ask if you could take them one of your pots of Christmas Cranberry Jam – make a special label for the jar to cheer them up. Or maybe they could come round to your home for a cup of tea and a crumpet with cranberry jam on top. Whatever you do this Christmas, remember to spread the joy!

WRAPPING UP THE YEAR

"There is a time for everything, and a season for every activity under the heavens."

(ECCLESIASTES 3, FOUND IN THE HEBREW *TANAKH* AND THE *BIBLE*)

So, it's time to say goodbye to the old and make way for the new. Maybe you'll make those New Year's resolutions all over again . . . and just maybe you'll do better at keeping them in 2023! Whatever you do, and wherever you are, thank you for reading this book and

HAPPY NEW YEAR TO YOU AND YOUR FRIENDS AND FAMILY!

CALENDAR 2022

JANUARY

Mo	Tu	We	Th	Fr	Sa	Su
					1	2
3	4	5	6	7	8	9
10	11	12	13	14	15	16
17	18	19	20	21	22	23
24	25	26	27	28	29	30
31						

Phases of the Moon

2: 9: 17: 25:

FEBRUARY

Mo	Tu	We	Th	Fr	Sa	Su
	1	2	3	4	5	6
7	8	9	10	11	12	13
14	15	16	17	18	19	20
21	22	23	24	25	26	27
28						

Phases of the Moon

1: 8: 16: 23:

MARCH

Mo	Tu	We	Th	Fr	Sa	Su
	1	2	3	4	5	6
7	8	9	10	11	12	13
14	15	16	17	18	19	20
21	22	23	24	25	26	27
28	29	30	31			

Phases of the Moon

2: 10: 18: 25:

APRIL

Mo	Tu	We	Th	Fr	Sa	Su
				1	2	3
4	5	6	7	8	9	10
11	12	13	14	15	16	17
18	19	20	21	22	23	24
25	26	27	28	29	30	

Phases of the Moon

1: 9: 16: 23: 30:

MAY

Mo	Tu	We	Th	Fr	Sa	Su
						1
2	3	4	5	6	7	8
9	10	11	12	13	14	15
16	17	18	19	20	21	22
23	24	25	26	27	28	29
30	31					

Phases of the Moon

9: 16: 22: 30:

JUNE

Mo	Tu	We	Th	Fr	Sa	Su
		1	2	3	4	5
6	7	8	9	10	11	12
13	14	15	16	17	18	19
20	21	22	23	24	25	26
27	28	29	30			

Phases of the Moon

7: 14: 21: 29:

JULY

Mo	Tu	We	Th	Fr	Sa	Su
				1	2	3
4	5	6	7	8	9	10
11	12	13	14	15	16	17
18	19	20	21	22	23	24
25	26	27	28	29	30	31

Phases of the Moon

7: 13: 20: 28:

AUGUST

Mo	Tu	We	Th	Fr	Sa	Su
1	2	3	4	5	6	7
8	9	10	11	12	13	14
15	16	17	18	19	20	21
22	23	24	25	26	27	28
29	30	31				

Phases of the Moon

5: 12: 19: 27:

SEPTEMBER

Mo	Tu	We	Th	Fr	Sa	Su
			1	2	3	4
5	6	7	8	9	10	11
12	13	14	15	16	17	18
19	20	21	22	23	24	25
26	27	28	29	30		

Phases of the Moon

3: 10: 17: 25:

OCTOBER

Mo	Tu	We	Th	Fr	Sa	Su
					1	2
3	4	5	6	7	8	9
10	11	12	13	14	15	16
17	18	19	20	21	22	23
24	25	26	27	28	29	30
31						

Phases of the Moon

3: 9: 17: 25:

NOVEMBER

Mo	Tu	We	Th	Fr	Sa	Su
	1	2	3	4	5	6
7	8	9	10	11	12	13
14	15	16	17	18	19	20
21	22	23	24	25	26	27
28	29	30				

Phases of the Moon

1: 8: 16: 23: 30:

DECEMBER

Mo	Tu	We	Th	Fr	Sa	Su
			1	2	3	4
5	6	7	8	9	10	11
12	13	14	15	16	17	18
19	20	21	22	23	24	25
26	27	28	29	30	31	

Phases of the Moon

8: 16: 23: 30:

NOTES

GLOSSARY

Advent The period leading up to Christmas

All Saints' Eve A Christian festival to remember saints and loved ones who have died

Allah The name of God for Muslims and Arab Christians

Anglo-Saxons People who lived in Great Britain from 410 until 1066

Apple Day A celebration of apples and orchards

April Fool's Day The first day of April, when people play jokes on each other

Ascension Day A Christian holy day to celebrate the day Jesus rose into heaven

Ash Wednesday The beginning of Lent

Beltane An ancient pagan festival that celebrates the return of summer

Bible The Christian holy book

Birth flower A flower linked to the month of a person's birth

Birthstone A precious or semi-precious stone linked to the month of a person's birth

Blue moon A second full moon in a calendar month

Burns Night A celebration of the Scottish poet Robert Burns

Cabinet A group of the most senior, or important, ministers in a government

Candlemas A Christian festival celebrating the first time that baby Jesus was taken to the temple

Catholic Someone who follows a branch of Christianity led by the Pope

Chinese New Year A colourful celebration of the start of the Chinese year, also known as the 'Spring Festival'

Christian Someone who follows the religion of Christianity and believes in God, Jesus Christ and the teachings of the *Bible*

Confetti Small pieces of paper traditionally thrown over the bride and groom at their wedding

Dairy Foods made from milk, including butter and cheese

Diwali A Hindu festival of lights to celebrate the victory of light over darkness

Easter A Christian festival to remember the death and return to life of Jesus Christ

Eid al-Adha Also known as the 'Sacrifice Feast', this Islamic festival honours Ibrahim's willingness to obey Allah and marks the end of the *Hajj* pilgrimage to Mecca

Eid al-Fitr Also known as the 'Festival of the Breaking of the Fast', this Islamic festival is a three-day celebration to mark the end of Ramadan

Epiphany A Christian holy day, held in January, which marks the end of the Christmas period

Equator An imaginary line drawn around the middle of the Earth at an equal distance from the north and south poles

Equinox The time twice a year when the length of day and night is exactly equal

Eta Aquariids A meteor shower formed by particles of dust left behind by Halley's Comet

Fast To spend a period of time without eating or drinking

Fertility The ability to create children or young

First-footing A Scottish New Year's tradition, where the 'first footer' is the first person to walk through the door after midnight

First quarter One quarter of the way through the moon's cycle, when we can see exactly half of the moon's face

Fossil The remains or traces of an ancient living thing that has been preserved in rock

Full moon When the entire face of the moon is lit up by the sun's rays

Ganesh Chaturthi A 10-day Hindu festival to worship the god Ganesha

Guy Fawkes A member of a group of English Catholics who tried to assassinate King James in 1604 by blowing up the Houses of Parliament

Hanukkah An eight-day 'festival of lights' celebrated by Jewish people, to remember how the Jewish army freed Jerusalem and took back the temple, which they re-dedicated to God

Harvest Gathering crops

Hemisphere Half of the Earth, divided into northern and southern hemispheres by the equator

Hieroglyphics The pictures and symbols that make up ancient Egyptian writing

Hobby horse A toy with a model of a horse's head at the end of a stick

Hogmanay The Scottish word for the last day of the year

Holi A Hindu spring festival in celebration of the god Krishna

Holy Spirit Christians believe God exists in three forms at the same time, as God in heaven, as Jesus Christ in heaven, and as the Holy Spirit, which is everywhere

House of Commons The British parliament, whose elected members make or change the country's laws

Imbolc A pagan festival marking the beginning of spring

Isra and Mi'raj An Islamic celebration of the Prophet Muhammad's journey from Mecca to Jerusalem and his journey into heaven, when Allah revealed to Muhammad that Muslims should pray five times a day

Jain Someone who follows the ancient Indian religion of Jainism that teaches *ahimsa* (non-violence) to all living creatures

Jerusalem The capital city of Israel, believed to be holy by Jewish people, Christians and Muslims

Jewish people Someone who follows the religion of Judaism and believes in God, the Hebrew prophets and the teachings of the *Torah*

Lammas A pagan celebration of the first harvest

Last quarter Three quarters of the way through the moon's cycle, when we can see exactly half of the moon's face

Lent A Christian period of fasting in the run-up to Easter

LGBT+ Lesbian, gay, bisexual, transgender plus any other sexual and gender identities

Litha The Anglo-Saxon word for midsummer

Lohri A Punjabi midwinter festival celebrated by Sikhs and Hindus

Lughnasadh A Gaelic festival celebrating the beginning of the harvest season

Maia The Greek goddess of fertility

May Day The first day of May, celebrated by dancing and singing

Mecca The holiest city of Islam

Meteor A fiery streak in the sky, created when dust and rocks from the tail of a comet pass through the Earth's atmosphere

Michaelmas A Christian festival held at the end of September to honour the angels

Midsummer The longest day and the shortest night of the year, also known as the summer solstice

Midwinter The shortest day and the longest night of the year, also known as the winter solstice

Migrate To move from one place to another

Mosque The Islamic place of worship

Muhammad The Muslim Prophet and founder of Islam

Muslim Someone who follows the religion of Islam and believes in Allah, the Prophet Muhammad, the five pillars of Islam and the teachings of the *Qur'an*

Natural remedy A medicine made using ingredients from nature

Neap tide A tide that happens twice a month, when the difference between high tide and low tide is at its lowest

New moon The first phase in the moon's cycle, when just a very thin crescent shape is visible at night

New Year's Honours The titles given to people by the Queen at New Year

Nymph The young, or larva, of some insects such as dragonflies

Old Testament The first part of the *Bible*, originally written in Hebrew

Ostara A pagan festival which is celebrated at the spring equinox

Pagan A follower of paganism, a pre-Christian religion, who believes in many gods and goddesses

Passover A Jewish celebration to remember how Moses helped the Israelites escape from Egypt

Pentecost A Christian festival on the seventh Sunday after Easter, to celebrate the day after his death when Jesus returned to his disciples in the form of the Holy Spirit

Promised Land The land that Jewish people believe was given by God to Abraham and his descendants

Purification The process of making something or someone clean

Purim A Jewish holiday in memory of when the Jewish people were saved from a cruel man called Haman

Qur'an The Islamic holy book

Raksha Bandhan A Hindu festival that celebrates the relationship between brothers and sisters

Ramadan A month when Muslims hold a fast during the hours of daylight to become closer to Allah, and to remember the time that the *Qur'an* was first revealed to the Prophet Muhammad

Resolution A decision to do, or not do something

Samhain Eve A pagan festival for giving thanks at the end of the harvest

Sea Sunday The day when Christians pray for sailors and their families

Shavuot A Jewish holiday to remember the day that God gave Moses the *Torah*

Shrove Tuesday The day before the Christian period of fasting called Lent begins, also known as 'Pancake Day'

Sikh Someone who follows the religion of Sikhism and believes in the writings and teachings of the Ten Sikh Gurus

Spring tide A tide just after a new or full moon, when the difference between high tide and low tide is at its highest

Sterilised Completely clean and free from germs. You can sterilise jam jars by washing them in hot, soapy water, or by heating them in the oven at 130°C for 20 minutes (ask an adult to help you)

Swan Upping An annual ceremony in which mute swans are taken from the River Thames to be counted and marked to identify them, before being released

Synagogue The Jewish place of worship

Ten Commandments A list of laws or rules that Christians and Jewish people follow that they believe were given by God to Moses

Tide The rising and falling of the sea

Torah The Jewish holy book

Trooping the colour A ceremony performed to celebrate the Queen's birthday

Tu B'Shevat Jewish New Year, also known as the 'New Year for Trees'

Twelfth Night A festival some Christians celebrate to mark the coming of the Epiphany

Wassailing A pagan tradition of blessing the apple trees in the new year

Whitsun Another name for the Christian festival of Pentecost

Yom Kippur A Jewish holiday for saying sorry for things you have done wrong and asking for forgiveness

Yule A pagan festival held in midwinter to celebrate the winter solstice

INDEX

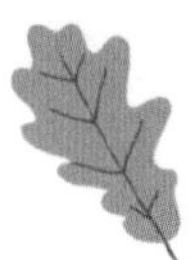